M000279406

ARCHITECT REGISTRATION EXAM

PROGRAMMING, PLANNING & PRACTICE

ARE SAMPLE PROBLEMS AND PRACTICE EXAM

SECOND EDITION

HOLLY WILLIAMS LEPPO, RA/CID
DAVID KENT BALLAST, FAIA

The Power to Pass®
www.ppi2pass.com

Professional Publications, Inc. • Belmont, California

Benefit by Registering This Book with PPI

- Get book updates and corrections.
- Hear the latest exam news.
- Obtain exclusive exam tips and strategies.
- Receive special discounts.

Register your book at **www.ppi2pass.com/register**.

Report Errors and View Corrections for This Book

PPI is grateful to every reader who notifies us of a possible error. Your feedback allows us to improve the quality and accuracy of our products. You can report errata and view corrections at **www.ppi2pass.com/errata**.

LEED® and USGBC® are registered trademarks of the U.S. Green Building Council.

MasterSpec® is a registered trademark of ARCOM.

**PROGRAMMING, PLANNING & PRACTICE:
ARE SAMPLE PROBLEMS AND PRACTICE EXAM
Second Edition**

Current printing of this edition: 2

Printing History

edition number	printing number	update
1	4	Minor corrections. Copyright update.
2	1	New edition. Code update. Copyright update.
2	2	Minor corrections.

Copyright © 2011 by Professional Publications, Inc. (PPI). All rights reserved. No part of this publication may be reproduced, stored in a retrieval system, or transmitted, in any form or by any means, electronic, mechanical, photocopying, recording, or otherwise, without the prior written permission of the publisher.

Printed in the United States of America.

PPI
1250 Fifth Avenue, Belmont, CA 94002
(650) 593-9119
www.ppi2pass.com

ISBN: 978-1-59126-327-2

Library of Congress Control Number: 2010941273

TABLE OF CONTENTS

PREFACE AND ACKNOWLEDGMENTS

This book is tailored to the needs of those studying for the Architect Registration Examination (ARE). For the second edition, we have updated the content to reflect the current *ARE 4.0 Guidelines*, as well as the most recent editions of a number of codes and standards, including

- 2005 *Americans with Disabilities Act and Architectural Barriers Act Accessibility Guidelines*
- 2007 AIA Contract Documents
- 2009 *International Building Code*

In the ARE, there is considerable overlap in what you need to study for the various divisions. For this reason, the *ARE Review Manual* covers all the divisions of the ARE in a single volume. This book, *Programming, Planning & Practice: ARE Sample Problems and Practice Exam*, is one of seven companion volumes, one for each ARE division. We believe that this organization will help you study for individual divisions most effectively.

You will find that this book and the related volumes are valuable parts of your exam preparation. Although there is no substitute for a good formal education and the broad-based experience provided by your internship with a practicing architect, this review series will help you direct your study efforts to increase your chances of passing the ARE.

Many people have helped in the production of this book. We would like to thank all the fine people at PPI including Scott Marley (project editor), Cathy Schrott (typesetter), Amy Schwertman (cover designer and illustrator), and Thomas Bergstrom (illustrator).

Although we had much help in preparing this new edition, the responsibility for any errors is our own. A current list of known errata for this book is maintained at **www.ppi2pass.com/errata**, and you can let us know of any errors you find at the same place. We greatly appreciate the time our readers take to help us keep this book accurate and up to date.

Holly Williams Leppo, RA/CID
David Kent Ballast, FAIA

INTRODUCTION

ABOUT THIS BOOK

Programming, Planning & Practice: ARE Sample Problems and Practice Exam is written to help you prepare for the Programming, Planning & Practice division of the Architect Registration Examination (ARE).

Although this book can be a valuable study aid by itself, it is designed to be used along with the *ARE Review Manual*, also published by PPI. The *ARE Review Manual* is organized into sections that cover all seven divisions of the ARE.

- Programming, Planning & Practice
- Site Planning & Design
- Schematic Design
- Structural Systems
- Building Systems
- Building Design & Construction Systems
- Construction Documents & Services

This book is one of seven companion volumes to the *ARE Review Manual* that PPI publishes. Each of these books contains sample problems and practice exams for one of the ARE divisions.

- *Programming, Planning & Practice: ARE Sample Problems and Practice Exam*
- *Site Planning & Design: ARE Sample Problems and Practice Exam*
- *Schematic Design: ARE Sample Problems and Practice Exam*
- *Structural Systems: ARE Sample Problems and Practice Exam*
- *Building Systems: ARE Sample Problems and Practice Exam*
- *Building Design & Construction Systems: ARE Sample Problems and Practice Exam*
- *Construction Documents & Services: ARE Sample Problems and Practice Exam*

THE ARCHITECT REGISTRATION EXAMINATION

Congratulations on completing (or nearing the end of) the Intern Development Program! You are two-thirds of the way to being able to call yourself an architect. NAAB degree? Check. IDP? Check. Now on to step three.

The final hurdle is the Architect Registration Examination. The ARE is a uniform test administered to candidates who wish to become licensed architects after they have served their required internships. It is given It is given throughout the United States, the U.S. territories, and Canada.

The ARE has been developed to protect the health, safety, and welfare of the public by testing a candidate's entry-level competence to practice architecture. Its content relates as closely as possible to situations encountered in practice. It tests for the kinds of knowledge, skills, and abilities required of an entry-level architect, with particular emphasis on those services that affect public health, safety, and welfare. In order to accomplish these objectives, the exam tests for

- knowledge in specific subject areas
- the ability to make decisions
- the ability to consolidate and use information to solve a problem
- the ability to coordinate the activities of others on the building team

The ARE also includes some professional practice and project management problems, and problems that are based on particular editions of codes as specified in the *ARE 4.0 Guidelines*. (However, the editions specified by the *ARE Guidelines* are not necessarily the most current editions available.)

The ARE is developed jointly by the National Council of Architectural Registration Boards (NCARB) and the Committee of Canadian Architectural Councils (CCAC), with the assistance of Prometric. Prometric serves as NCARB's test development and operations consultant, and Prometric operates and maintains the test centers where the ARE is administered.

Although the responsibility of professional licensing rests with each individual state, every state's board requires successful completion of the ARE to achieve registration or licensure. One of the primary reasons for a uniform test is to facilitate reciprocity—that is, to enable an architect to more easily gain a license to practice in states other than the one in which he or she was originally licensed.

The ARE is administered and graded entirely by computer. All divisions of the exam are offered six days a week at a network of test centers across North America. The results are scored by computer, and the results are forwarded to individual state boards of architecture, which process them and send them to candidates. If you fail a division, you must wait six months before you can retake that division.

First Steps

As you begin to prepare for the exam, you should first obtain a current copy of the *ARE Guidelines* from NCARB. This booklet will get you started with the exam process and will be a valuable reference throughout. It includes descriptions of the seven divisions, instructions on how to apply, pay for, and take the ARE, and other useful information. You can download a PDF version at www.ncarb.org, or you can request a printed copy through the contact information provided at that site.

The NCARB website also gives current information about the exam, education requirements, training, examination procedures, and NCARB reciprocity services. It includes sample scenarios of the computer-based examination process and examples of costs associated with taking the computer-based exam.

The PPI website is also a good source of answers to frequently asked questions about the exam (at **www.ppi2pass.com/arefaq**).

To register as an examinee, you should obtain the registration requirements from the board in the state, province, or territory where you want to be registered. The exact requirements vary from one jurisdiction to another, so contact your local board. Links to state boards can be found at **www.ppi2pass.com/faqs/architecture-state-boards**.

As soon as NCARB has verified your qualifications and you have received your "Authorization to Test" letter, you may begin scheduling examinations. The exams are offered on a first come, first served basis and must be scheduled at least 72 hours in advance. See the *ARE Guidelines* for instructions on finding a current list of testing centers. You may take the

exams at any location, even outside the state in which you intend to become registered.

You may schedule any division of the ARE at any time and may take the divisions in any order. Divisions can be taken one at a time, to spread out preparation time and exam costs, or can be taken together in any combination.

However, you must pass all seven divisions of the ARE within a single five-year period. This period, or "rolling clock," begins on the date of the first division you passed. If you have not completed the ARE within five years, the divisions that you passed more than five years ago are no longer credited, and the content in them must be retaken. Your new five-year period begins on the date of the earliest division you passed within the last five years.

Examination Format

The ARE is organized into seven divisions that test various areas of architectural knowledge and problem-solving ability.

Programming, Planning & Practice

85 multiple-choice problems
1 graphic vignette: Site Zoning

Site Planning & Design

65 multiple-choice problems
2 graphic vignettes: Site Design, Site Grading

Schematic Design

2 graphic vignettes: Building Layout, Interior Layout

Structural Systems

125 multiple-choice problems
1 graphic vignette: Structural Layout

Building Systems

95 multiple-choice problems
1 graphic vignette: Mechanical & Electrical Plan

Building Design & Construction Systems

85 multiple-choice problems
3 graphic vignettes: Accessibility/Ramp, Roof Plan, Stair Design

Construction Documents & Services

100 multiple-choice problems
1 graphic vignette: Building Section

Experienced test-takers will tell you that there is quite a bit of overlap among these divisions. Problems that seem better suited to the Construction Documents & Services division may show up on the Building Design & Construction Systems division, for example, and problems on architectural history and building regulations might show up anywhere. That's why it's important to have a comprehensive strategy for studying and taking the exams.

The ARE is given entirely by computer. There are two kinds of problems on the exam. Multiple-choice problems are short questions presented on the computer screen; you answer them by clicking on the right answer or answers, or by filling in a blank. Graphic vignettes are longer problems in design; you solve a vignette by planning and drawing your solution on the computer. Six of the seven divisions contain both multiple-choice sections and graphic vignettes; the Schematic Design division contains only vignettes. Both kinds of problems are described later in this Introduction.

STUDY GUIDELINES

After the five to seven years (or even more) of higher education you've received to this point, you probably have a good idea of the study strategy that works best for you. The trick is figuring out how to apply that to the ARE. Unlike many college courses, there isn't a textbook or set of class notes from which all the exam problems will be derived. The exams are very broad and draw problems from multiple areas of knowledge.

The first challenge, then, is figuring out what to study. The ARE is never quite the same exam twice. The field of knowledge tested is always the same, but the specific problems asked are drawn randomly from a large pool, and will differ from one candidate to the next. One division may contain many code-related problems for one candidate and only a few for the next. This makes the ARE a challenge to study for.

The *ARE Guidelines* contain a link to lists of resources recommended by NCARB. These lists can seem overwhelming, though, and on top of that, many of the recommended books are expensive or no longer in print. To help address this problem, PPI has published the *ARE Review Manual*, which gives you an overview of the concepts and information that will be most useful in preparing for the ARE. A list of helpful resources for preparing for the Programming, Planning & Practice division can also be found in the Recommended Reading section of this book.

Your method of studying for the ARE should be based on both the content and form of the exam and on your school and work experience. Because the exam covers such a broad range of subject matter, it cannot possibly include every detail of practice. Rather, it tends to focus on what is considered entry-level knowledge and knowledge that is important for the protection of the public's health, safety, and welfare. Other types of problems are asked, too, but this knowledge should be the focus of your review schedule.

Your recent work experience should also help you determine what areas to study the most. If, for example, you have been working with construction documents for several years, you will probably need less review in that area than in others you have not had much recent experience with.

The *ARE Review Manual* and its companion volumes are structured to help you focus on the topics that are more likely to be included in the exam in one form or another. Some subjects may seem familiar or may be easy to recall from memory, and others may seem completely foreign; the latter are the ones to give particular attention to. It may be wise to study additional sources on these subjects, take review seminars, or get special help from someone who is knowledgeable in the topic.

A typical candidate might spend about forty hours preparing for and taking each exam. Some will need to study more, some less. Forty hours is about one week of studying eight hours a day, or two weeks of four hours a day, or a month of two hours a day, along with reasonable breaks and time to attend to other responsibilities. As you probably work full time and have other family and personal obligations, it is important to develop a realistic schedule and do your best to stick to it. The ARE is not the kind of exam you can cram for the night before.

Also, since the fees are high and retaking a test is expensive, you want to do your best and pass in as few tries as possible. Allowing enough time to study and going into each exam well prepared will help you relax and concentrate on the problems.

The following steps may provide a useful structure for an exam study program.

Step 1: Start early. You can't review for a test like this by starting two weeks before the date. This is especially true if you are taking all portions of the exam for the first time.

Step 2: Go through the *ARE Review Manual* quickly to get a feeling for the scope of the subject matter and how the major topics are organized. Whatever division you're studying for, plan to review the chapters on building regulations as well. Review the *ARE Guidelines*.

Step 3: Based on your review of the *ARE Review Manual* and *ARE Guidelines*, and on a realistic appraisal of your strong and weak areas, set priorities for study and determine which topics need more study time.

Step 4: Divide review subjects into manageable units and organize them into a sequence of study. It is generally best to start with the less familiar subjects. Based on the exam date and plans for beginning study, assign a time limit to each study unit. Again, your knowledge of a subject should determine the time devoted to it. You may want to devote an entire week to earthquake design if it is an unfamiliar subject, and only one day to timber design if it is a familiar one. In setting up a schedule, be realistic about other life commitments as well as your personal ability to concentrate on studying over a length of time.

Step 5: Begin studying, and stick with the schedule. Of course, this is the most difficult part of the process and the one that requires the most self-discipline. The job should be easier if you have started early and if you are following a realistic schedule that allows time for recreation and personal commitments.

Step 6: Stop studying a day or two before the exam. Relax. By this time, no amount of additional cramming will help.

At some point in your studying, you will want to spend some time becoming familiar with the program you will be using to solve the graphic vignettes, which does not resemble commercial CAD software. The software and sample vignettes can be downloaded from the NCARB website at www.ncarb.org.

There are many schools of thought on the best order for taking the divisions. One factor to consider is the six-month waiting period before you can retake a particular division. It's never fun to predict what you might fail, but if you know that a specific area might give you trouble, consider taking that exam near the beginning. You might be pleasantly surprised when you check the mailbox, but if not, as you work through the rest of the exams, the clock will be ticking and you can schedule the retest six months later.

Here are some additional tips.

- Learn concepts first, and then details later. For example, it is much better to understand the basic ideas and theories of waterproofing than it is to attempt to memorize dozens of waterproofing products and details. Once the concept is clear, the details are much easier to learn and to apply during the exam.

- Use the *ARE Review Manual's* index to focus on particular subjects in which you feel weak, especially subjects that can apply to more than one division.

- Don't tackle all your hardest subjects first. Make one of your early exams one that you feel fairly confident about. It's nice to get off on the right foot with a PASS.

- Programming, Planning & Practice and Building Design & Construction Systems both tend to be "catch-all" divisions that cover a lot of material from the Construction Documents & Services division as well as others. Consider taking Construction Documents & Services first among those three, and then the other two soon after.

- Many past candidates recommend taking the Programming, Planning & Practice division last or nearly last, so that you will be familiar with the body of knowledge for all the other divisions as well.

- Brush up on architectural history before taking any of the divisions with multiple-choice sections. Know major buildings and their architects, particularly structures that are representative of an architect's philosophy (for example, Le Corbusier and the Villa Savoye) or that represent "firsts" or "turning points."

- Try to schedule your exams so that you'll have enough time to get yourself ready, eat, and review a little. If you'll have a long drive to the testing center, try to avoid having to make it during rush hour.

- If you are planning to take more than one division at a time, do not overstudy any one portion of the exam. It is generally better to review the concepts than to try to become an overnight expert in one area. For example, you may need to know general facts about plate girders, but you will not need to know how to complete a detailed design of a plate girder.

- Even though you may have a good grasp of the information and knowledge in a particular subject area, be prepared to address problems on the material in a variety of forms and from different points of view. For example, you may have studied and know definitions, but you will also need to be able to apply that knowledge when a problem includes a definition-type word as part of a more complex situation-type of problem.

- Solve as many sample problems as possible, including those provided with NCARB's practice program, the books of sample problems and practice exams published by PPI, and any others that are available.

- Take advantage of the community of intern architects going through this experience with you. Some local AIA chapters offer ARE preparation courses or may be able to help you organize a study group with other interns in your area. PPI's Passing Zones are interactive online reviews to help you prepare for individual divisions of the ARE. Find out more at **www.ppi2pass.com/passingzone**.

Visit website forums to discuss the exam with others who have taken it or are preparing to take it. The Architecture Exam Forum at **www.ppi2pass.com/areforum** is a great online resource for questions, study advice, and encouragement. Even though the special problems on the ARE change daily, it is a good idea to get a feeling for the ARE's format, its general emphasis, and the subject areas that previous candidates have found particularly troublesome.

- A day or two before the first test session, stop studying in order to relax as much as possible. Get plenty of sleep the night before the test.

- Try to relax as much as possible during study periods and during the exam itself. Worrying is counterproductive. Candidates who have worked diligently in school, have obtained a wide range of experience during internship, and have started exam review early will be in the best possible position to pass the ARE.

TAKING THE EXAM

What to Bring

Bring multiple forms of photo ID and your Authorization to Test letter to the test site.

It is neither necessary nor permitted to bring any reference materials or scratch paper into the test site. Pencils and scratch paper are provided by the proctor and must be returned when leaving the exam room. Earplugs will also be provided. Leave all your books and notes in the car. Most testing centers have lockers for your keys, small personal belongings, and cell phone.

Do not bring a calculator into the test site. A calculator built into the testing software will be available in all divisions.

Arriving at the Testing Center

Allow plenty of time to get to the exam site, to avoid transportation problems such as getting lost or stuck in traffic jams. If you can, arrive a little early, and take a little time in the parking lot to review one last time the formulas and other things you need to memorize. Then relax, take a few deep breaths, and go take the exam.

Once at the test site, you will check in with the attendant, who will verify your identification and your Authorization to Test. (Don't forget to take this home with you after each exam; you'll need it for the next one.) After you check in, you'll be shown to your testing station.

When the exam begins, you will have the opportunity to click through a tutorial that explains how the computer program works. You'll probably want to read through it the first time, but after that initial exam, you will know how the software works and you won't need the tutorial. Take a deep breath, organize your paper and pencils, and take advantage of the opportunity to dump all the facts floating around in your brain onto your scratch paper—write down as much as you can.

This includes formulas, ratios ("if x increases, y decreases"), and so on—anything that you are trying desperately not to forget. If you can get all the things you've crammed at the last minute onto that paper, you'll be able to think a little more clearly about the problems posed on the screen.

Taking the Multiple-Choice Sections

The ARE multiple-choice sections include several types of problems.

One type of multiple-choice problem is based on written, graphic, or photographic information. You will need to examine the information and select the correct answer from four given options. Some problems may require calculations.

A second type of multiple-choice problem lists four or five items or statements, which are given Roman numerals from I to IV or I to V. For example, the problem may give five statements about a subject, and you must choose the statements that are true. The four answer choices are combinations of these numerals, such as "I and III" or "II, IV, and V."

A third type of multiple-choice problem describes a situation that could be encountered in actual practice. Drawings, diagrams, photographs, forms, tables, or other data may also be given. The problem requires you to select the best answer from four options.

Two kinds of problems that NCARB calls "alternate item types" also show up in the multiple-choice sections. In a "fill in the blank" problem, you must fill a blank with a number derived from a table or calculation. In a "check all that apply" problem, six options are given, and you must choose all the correct answers. The problem tells how many of the options are correct, from two to four. You must choose all the correct answers to receive credit; partial credit is not given.

Between 10% and 15% of the problems in a multiple-choice section will be these "alternate item type" problems. Every problem on the ARE, however, counts the same toward your total score.

Keep in mind that multiple-choice problems often require the examinee to do more than just select an answer based on memory. At times it will be necessary to combine several facts, analyze data, perform a calculation, or review a drawing. You will probably not need the entire time allotted for the multiple-choice sections. If you have time for more than one pass through the problems, you can make good use of it.

Here are some tips for the multiple-choice problems.

- Go through the entire section in one somewhat swift pass, answering the problems that you're sure about and marking the others so you can return to them later. If a problem requires calculations, skip it for now unless it's very simple. Then go back to the beginning and work your way through the exam again, taking a little more time to read each problem and think through the answer.

- Another benefit of going through the entire section at the beginning is that occasionally there is information in one problem that may help you answer another problem somewhere else.

- If you are very unsure of a problem, pick your best answer, mark it, and move on. You will probably have time at the end of the test to go back and recheck these answers. But remember, your first response is usually the best.

- Always answer all the problems. Unanswered problems are counted wrong, so even if you are just guessing, it's better to choose an answer and have a chance of it being correct than to skip it and be certain of getting it wrong. When faced with four options, the old SAT strategy of eliminating the two options that are definitely wrong and making your best guess between the two that remain is helpful on the ARE, too.

- Some problems may seem too simple. Although a few very easy and obvious problems are included on the ARE, more often the simplicity should serve as a red flag to warn you to reevaluate the problem for exceptions to a rule or special circumstances that make the obvious, easy response incorrect.

- Watch out for absolute words in a problem, such as "always," "never," and "completely." These are often a clue that some little exception exists, turning what reads like a true statement into a false one or vice versa.

- Be alert for words like "seldom," "usually," "best," and "most reasonable." These indicate that some judgment will be involved in answering the problem. Look for two or more options that appear to be very similar.

- Some divisions will provide an on-screen reference sheet with useful formulas and other information that will help you solve some problems. Skim through the reference sheet so you know what information is there, and then use it as a resource.

- Occasionally there may be a defective problem. This does not happen very often, but if it does, make the best choice possible under the circumstances. Flawed problems are usually discovered, and either they are not counted on the test or any one of the correct answers is credited.

Solving the Vignettes

Each of the eleven graphic vignettes on the ARE is designed to test a particular area of knowledge and skill. Each one presents a base plan of some kind and gives programmatic and other requirements. You must create a plan that satisfies the requirements. There is one Programming, Planning & Practice vignette.

In the *Site Zoning* vignette, the candidate must draw on a site plan the areas suitable for surface improvements and building construction, taking into account limitations imposed by zoning, setback, and other regulatory and programmatic requirements. On a corresponding grid, the candidate must draw the profile of the contour lines indicated on the site plan, and draw a profile line showing the maximum buildable envelope.

The computer scores the vignettes by a complex grading method. Design criteria are given various point values, and responses are categorized as Acceptable, Unacceptable, or Indeterminate.

General Tips for the Vignette

Here are some general tips for approaching the vignette. More detailed solving tips can be found in the vignette solution in this book.

- Remember that with the current format and computer grading, each vignette covers only a very specific area of knowledge and offers a limited number of possible solutions. In a few cases only one solution is really possible. Use this as an advantage.

- Read everything thoroughly, twice. Follow the requirements exactly, letting each problem solve itself as much as possible. Be careful not to read more into the instructions than is there. The test writers are very specific about what they want; there is no need to add to the vignette requirements. If a particular type of solution is strongly suggested, follow that lead.

- Consider only those code requirements given in the vignette, even if they deviate from familiar codes. Do not read anything more into the vignette. The code requirements may be slightly different from what you use in practice.

- Use the scratch paper provided to sketch possible solutions before starting the final solution.

- Make sure all programmed elements are included in the final design.

- When the functional requirements of the vignette have been solved, use the vignette directions as a checklist to make sure all criteria have been satisfied.

General Tips for Using the Vignette Software

It is important to practice with the vignette software that will be used in the exam. The program is unique to the ARE and unlike standard CAD software. If you are unfamiliar with the software interface you will waste valuable time learning to use it, and are likely to run out of time before completing the vignettes. Practice software can be downloaded at no charge from NCARB's website at www.ncarb.org. Usage time for the practice program can also be purchased at Prometric test centers. The practice software includes tutorials, directions, and one practice vignette for each of the eleven vignettes.

Here are some general tips for using the vignette software.

- When elements overlap on the screen, it may be difficult to select a particular element. If this happens, repeatedly click on the element without moving the mouse until the desired element is highlighted.

- Try to stay in "ortho" mode. This mode can be used to solve most vignettes, and it makes the solution process much easier and quicker. Unless obviously required by the vignette, creating additional angles only complicates things and eats up your limited time.

- If the vignette relates to contour modifications, it may help to draw schematic sections through the significant existing slopes. This provides a three-dimensional image of the situation.

- When drawing, if the program states that elements should connect, make sure they touch at their boundaries only and do not overlap. Use the *check* tool to determine if there are any overlaps. Walls that do not align correctly can cause a solution to be downgraded or even rejected. Remember, walls between spaces change color temporarily when properly aligned.

- Make liberal use of the *zoom* tool for sizing and aligning components accurately. Zoom in as closely as possible on the area being worked. When aligning objects, it is also helpful to use the full-screen cursor.

- Turn on the grid and verify spacing. This makes it easier to align objects and get a sense of the sizes of objects and the distances between them. Use the *measure* tool to check exact measurements if needed.

- Make liberal use of the sketch tools. These can be turned on and off and do not count during the grading, but they can be used to show relationships and for temporary guidelines and other notations.

- Use sketch circles to show required distances, setbacks, clearances, and similar measures.

AFTER THE EXAM

When you've clicked the button to end the test, the computer may prompt you to provide some demographic information about yourself and your education and experience. Then gather your belongings, turn in your scratch paper and materials—you must leave them with the proctor—and leave the test site. (For security reasons, you can't remove anything from the test site.) If the staff has retained your Authorization to Test and your identification, don't forget to retrieve both.

If you should encounter any problems during the exam or have any concerns, be sure to report them to the test site administrator and to NCARB as soon as possible. If you wait longer than ten days after you test, NCARB will not respond to your complaint. You must report your complaint immediately and directly to NCARB and copy your state registration board for any hope of assistance.

Then it's all over but the wait for the mail. How long it takes to get your scores will vary with the efficiency of your state registration board, which reviews the scores from NCARB before passing along the results. But four to six weeks is typical.

As you may have heard from classmates and colleagues, the ARE is a difficult exam—but it is certainly not impossible to pass. A solid architectural education and a well-rounded internship are the best preparation you can have. Watch carefully and listen to the vocabulary used by architects with more experience. Look for opportunities to participate in all phases of project delivery so that you have some "real world" experience to apply to the scenarios you will inevitably find on the exam.

One last piece of advice is not to put off taking the exams. Take them as soon as you become eligible. You will probably still remember a little bit from your college courses and you may even have your old textbooks and notes handy. As life gets more complicated—with spouses and children and work obligations—it is easy to make excuses and never find time to get around to it. Make the commitment, and do it now. After all, this is the last step to reaching your goal of calling yourself an architect.

HOW TO USE THIS BOOK

This book contains 88 sample multiple-choice problems and one sample vignette, as well as one complete practice exam consisting of 85 multiple-choice problems and one vignette. These have been written to help you prepare for the Programming, Planning & Practice division of the Architect Registration Examination (ARE).

One of the best ways to prepare for the ARE is by solving sample problems. While you are studying for this division, use the sample problems in this book to make yourself familiar with the different types of problems and the breadth of topics you are likely to encounter on the actual exam. Then when it's time to take the ARE, you will already be comfortable with the format of the exam problems. Also, seeing which sample problems you can and cannot answer correctly will help you gauge your understanding of the topics covered in the Programming, Planning & Practice division.

The sample multiple-choice problems in this book are organized by subject area, so that you can concentrate on one subject at a time if you like. Each problem is immediately followed by its answer and an explanation.

The sample vignette in this book can be solved directly on the base plan provided or on a sheet of tracing paper. Alternatively, you can download an electronic file of the base plan in PDF format from **www.ppi2pass.com/vignettes** for use in your own CAD program. (On the actual exam, the vignette is solved on the computer using NCARB's own software; see the Introduction for more information about this.) When you are finished with your solution to the vignette, compare it against the sample passing and failing solutions that follow.

While the sample problems in this book are intended for you to use as you study for the exam, the practice exam is best used only when you have almost finished your study of the Programming, Planning & Practice topics. A week or two before you are scheduled to take the division, when you

feel you are nearly ready for the exam, do a "dry run" by taking the practice exam in this book. This will hone your test-taking skills and give you a reality check about how prepared you really are.

The experience will be most valuable to you if you treat the practice exam as though it were an actual exam. Do not read the problems ahead of time and do not look at the solutions until after you've finished. Try to simulate the exam experience as closely as possible. This means locking yourself away in a quiet space, setting an alarm for the exam's testing time, and working through the entire practice exam with no coffee, television, or telephone—only your calculator, a pencil, your drafting tools or CAD program for the vignettes, and a few sheets of scratch paper. (On the actual exam, the CAD program, an on-screen calculator, scratch paper, and pencils are provided.) This will help you prepare to budget your time, give you an idea of what the actual exam experience will be like, and help you develop a test-taking strategy that works for you.

The target times for the two sections of the practice exam are

Multiple choice: 2 hours

Site Zoning Vignette: 1 hour

Record your answers for the multiple-choice section of the practice exam using the "bubble" answer form at the front of the exam. When you are finished, you can check your answers quickly against the filled-in answer key at the front of the Solutions section. Then turn to the solutions and read the explanations of the answers, especially those you answered incorrectly. The explanation will give you a better understanding of the intent of the problem and why individual options are right or wrong.

The Solutions section may also be used as a guide for the final phase of your studies. As opposed to a traditional study guide that is organized into chapters and paragraphs of facts, this problem-and-solution format can help you see how the exam might address a topic, and what types of problems you are likely to encounter. If you still are not clear about a particular subject after reading a solution's explanation, review the subject in one of your study resources. Give yourself time for further study, and then take the multiple-choice section again.

The vignette portion of the practice exam can be solved the same way as the sample vignette, either directly on the base plan, on tracing paper, or with a CAD program using the electronic file downloaded from **www.ppi2pass.com/ vignettes**. Try to solve the vignette within the target time given. When you are finished, compare your drawing against the passing and failing solutions given in the Solutions section.

This book is best used in conjunction with your primary study source or study guide, such as PPI's *ARE Review Manual*. *Programming, Planning & Practice: ARE Sample Problems and Practice Exam* is not intended to give you all the information you will need to pass this division of the ARE. Rather, it is designed to expose you to a variety of problem types and to help you sharpen your problem-solving and test-taking skills. With a sound review and the practice you'll get from this book, you'll be well on your way to successfully passing the Programming, Planning & Practice division of the Architect Registration Examination.

HOW SI UNITS ARE USED IN THIS BOOK

This book includes equivalent measurements in the text and illustrations using the Système International (SI), or the *metric system* as it is commonly called. However, the use of SI units for construction and book publishing in the United States is problematic. This is because the building construction industry in the United States (with the exception of federal construction) has generally not adopted the metric system. As a result, equivalent measurements of customary U.S. units (also called English or inch-pound units) are usually given as a *soft* conversion, in which customary U.S. measurements are simply converted into SI units using standard conversion factors. This always results in a number with excessive significant digits. When construction is done using SI units, the building is designed and drawn according to *hard* conversions, where planning dimensions and building products are based on a metric module from the beginning. For example, studs are spaced 400 mm on center to accommodate panel products that are manufactured in standard 1200 mm widths.

During the present time of transition to the Système International in the United States, code-writing bodies, federal laws such as the ADA and the ABA, product manufacturers, trade associations, and other construction-related industries typically still use the customary U.S. system and make soft conversions to develop SI equivalents. Some manufacturers produce the same products in sizes for each measuring system. Although there are industry standards for developing SI equivalents, there is no perfect consistency for rounding off when conversions are made. For example, the *International Building Code* shows a 152 mm equivalent when a 6 in dimension is required, while the *Americans with Disabilities Act and Architectural Barriers Act Accessibility Guidelines* (*ADA/ABA Guidelines*) give a 150 mm equivalent for the same customary U.S. dimension.

To further complicate matters, each book publisher may employ a slightly different house style in handling SI equivalents when customary U.S. units are used as the primary measuring system. The confusion is likely to continue until the United States construction industry adopts the SI system completely, eliminating the need for dual dimensioning in publishing.

For the purposes of this book, the following conventions have been adopted.

Throughout the book, the customary U.S. measurements are given first with the SI equivalent shown in parentheses. When the measurement is millimeters, units are not shown. For example, a dimension may be indicated as 4 ft 8 in (1422). When the SI equivalent is some other unit, such as for volume or area, the units are indicated. For example, 250 ft^2 (23 m^2).

Following standard conventions, all SI distance measurements in illustrations are in millimeters unless specifically indicated as meters.

When a measurement is given as part of a problem scenario, the SI measurement is not necessarily meant to be roughly equal to the U.S. measurement. For example, a hypothetical force on a beam might be given as 12 kips (12 kN). 12 kips is actually equal to about 53.38 kN, but the intention in such cases is only to provide two problems, one in U.S. units and one in SI units, of about the same difficulty. Solve the entire problem in either U.S. or SI units; don't try to convert from one to the other in the middle of solving a problem.

When dimensions are for informational use, the SI equivalent rounded to the nearest millimeter is used.

When dimensions are given and they relate to planning or design guidelines, the SI equivalent is rounded to the nearest 5 mm for numbers over a few inches and to the nearest 10 mm for numbers over a few feet. When the dimension exceeds several feet, the number is rounded to the nearest 100 mm. For example, if you need a space about 10 ft wide for a given activity, the modular, rounded SI equivalent will be given as 3000 mm. More exact conversions are not required.

When an item is only manufactured to a customary U.S. measurement, the nearest SI equivalent rounded to the nearest millimeter is given, unless the dimension is very small (as for metal gages), in which case a more precise decimal equivalent will be given. Some materials, such as glass, are often manufactured to SI sizes. So, for example, a nominal $\frac{1}{2}$ in thick piece of glass will have an SI equivalent of 13 mm but can be ordered as 12 mm.

When there is a hard conversion in the industry and an SI equivalent item is manufactured, the hard conversion is given. For example, a 24 × 24 ceiling tile would have the hard conversion of 600 × 600 (instead of 610) because these are manufactured and available in the United States.

When an SI conversion is used by a code, such as the *International Building Code*, or published in another regulation, such as the *ADA/ABA Guidelines*, the SI equivalents used by the issuing agency are printed in this book. For example, the same 10 ft dimension given previously as 3000 mm for a planning guideline would have an SI equivalent of 3048 mm in the context of the IBC because this is what that code requires. The *ADA/ABA Guidelines* generally follow the rounding rule, to take SI dimensions to the nearest 10 mm. For example, a 10 ft requirement for accessibility will be shown as 3050 mm. The code requirements for readers outside the United States may be slightly different.

This book uses different abbreviations for pounds of force and pounds of mass in customary U.S. units. The abbreviation used for pounds of force (pounds-force) is lbf, and the abbreviation used for pounds of mass (pounds-mass) is lbm.

CODES AND STANDARDS
USED IN THIS BOOK

ADA/ABA Guidelines: *Americans with Disabilities Act and Architectural Barriers Act Accessibility Guidelines*, 2005. U.S. Architectural and Transportation Barriers Compliance Board, Washington, DC.

AIA: Contract Documents, 2007. American Institute of Architects, Washington, DC.

ANSI/BOMA Z65.1-2010: *Office Buildings: Standard Methods of Measurement*, 2010. Building Owners and Managers Association, Washington, DC.

IBC: *International Building Code*, 2009. International Code Council, Washington, DC.

The Secretary of the Interior's Standards for Rehabilitation and Illustrated Guidelines for Rehabilitating Historic Buildings, 1995. U.S. Department of the Interior, Washington, DC.

RECOMMENDED READING

General Reference

ARCOM. *MasterSpec*. Salt Lake City: ARCOM. (Familiarity with the format and language of specifications is very helpful.)

ARCOM and American Institute of Architects. *The Graphic Standards Guide to Architectural Finishes: Using MasterSpec to Evaluate, Select, and Specify Materials*. Hoboken, NJ: John Wiley & Sons.

Ballast, David Kent, and Steven E. O'Hara. *ARE Review Manual*. Belmont, CA: Professional Publications, Inc..

Fitch, James Marston. *Historic Preservation: Curatorial Management of the Built World*. Charlottesville: University Press of Virginia.

Guthrie, Pat. *Architect's Portable Handbook*. New York: McGraw-Hill.

Harris, Cyril M., ed. *Dictionary of Architecture and Construction*. New York: McGraw-Hill.

Mahoney, William D. *ADA/ABA Handbook: Accessibility Guidelines for Buildings and Facilities*. East Providence, RI: BNI Building News.

Ramsey, Charles G., and Harold R. Sleeper. *Architectural Graphic Standards*. Hoboken, NJ: John Wiley & Sons. (The student edition is an acceptable substitute for the professional version.)

U.S. Green Building Council. *LEED Reference Package for New Construction and Major Renovations*. Washington, DC: U.S. Green Building Council.

Programming, Planning & Practice

Ambrose, James. *Subsurface Conditions*. Washington, DC: National Council of Architectural Registration Boards.

Ambrose, James, and Peter Brandow. *Simplified Site Design*. Hoboken, NJ: John Wiley & Sons.

Beall, Christine, and Deborah Slaton. *Guide to Preparing Design and Construction Documents for Historic Projects* (TD-2-8). Alexandria, VA: Construction Specifications Institute and Association for Preservation Technology International.

Brown, G. Z., and Mark DeKay. *Sun, Wind, and Light*. Hoboken, NJ: John Wiley & Sons.

Demkin, Joseph A., ed. *Architect's Handbook of Professional Practice* by the American Institute of Architects. New York: John Wiley & Sons. (The student edition is an acceptable substitute for the professional version.)

Givoni, Baruch. Climate *Considerations in Building and Urban Design*. Hoboken, NJ: John Wiley & Sons.

Katz, Peter. *The New Urbanism: Toward an Architecture of Community*. New York: McGraw-Hill.

Kostof, Spiro. *A History of Architecture: Settings and Rituals*. New York: Oxford University Press.

Kostof, Spiro, and Richard Tobias. *The City Assembled: The Elements of Urban Form Through History*. Boston, MA: Bulfinch Press.

Kumlin, Robert R. *Architectural Programming: Creative Techniques for Design Professionals*. New York: McGraw-Hill, Inc.

Lynch, Kevin. *The Image of the City*. Cambridge, MA: MIT Press.

Lynch, Kevin, and Gary Hack. *Site Planning*. Cambridge, MA: MIT Press.

McHarg, Ian L. *Design with Nature*. Hoboken, NJ: John Wiley & Sons.

Newman, Oscar. *Creating Defensible Space*. Washington, DC: U.S. Department of Housing and Urban Development. (Download from www.defensiblespace.com.)

Olgyay, Victor. *Design with Climate*. New York: Van Nostrand Reinhold.

Parker, Harry, John W. MacGuire, and James Ambrose. *Simplified Site Engineering*. Hoboken, NJ: John Wiley & Sons.

Peña, William, and Steven A. Parshall. *Problem Seeking: An Architectural Programming Primer*. Hoboken, NJ: John Wiley & Sons.

U.S. Department of Energy and Public Technology, Inc. *Sustainable Building Technical Manual: Green Building Design, Construction, and Operations*. Washington, DC: Public Technology, Inc.

Graphic Vignettes

Allen, Edward, and Joseph Iano. *The Architect's Studio Companion: Rules of Thumb for Preliminary Design*. Hoboken, NJ: John Wiley & Sons.

Ambrose, James, and Peter Brandow. *Simplified Site Design*. Hoboken, NJ: John Wiley & Sons.

Ching, Francis D.K., and Steven R. Winkel. *Building Codes Illustrated: A Guide to Understanding the International Building Code*. Hoboken, NJ: John Wiley & Sons.

Hoke, John Ray, ed. *Architectural Graphic Standards*. Hoboken, NJ: John Wiley & Sons.

Karlen, Mark. *Space Planning Basics*. Hoboken, NJ: John Wiley & Sons.

Parker, Harry, John W. MacGuire, and James Ambrose. *Simplified Site Engineering*. Hoboken, NJ: John Wiley & Sons.

Architectural History

(Brush up on this before taking any of the multiple-choice exams, as architectural history problems are scattered throughout the sections.)

Curtis, William J.R. *Modern Architecture Since 1900*. London: Phaedon Press, Ltd.

Frampton, Kenneth. *Modern Architecture: A Critical History*. London: Thames and Hudson.

Trachtenberg, Marvin, and Isabelle Hyman. *Architecture: From Pre-History to Post-Modernism*. Englewood Cliffs, NJ: Prentice-Hall.

SAMPLE PROBLEMS

PROGRAMMING AND ANALYSIS

1. The height of a proposed building would be most influenced by the decision to use

    A. daylighting
    B. indirect lighting
    C. underfloor ventilation systems
    D. interstitial spaces

Solution

Interstitial spaces between occupied floors require the most additional height per floor and the most total building height because they must be high enough to accommodate a person accessing the space for maintenance duties, as well as the ducts and equipment servicing the occupied spaces below.

Daylighting, indirect lighting, and underfloor ventilation systems would add only a few feet, at most, to each floor.

The answer is D.

2. The historic concept of formality could be most readily conveyed in a contemporary building through the use of

    A. rhythm
    B. symmetry
    C. proportion
    D. emphasis

Solution

Throughout the history of architecture, symmetry has been one of the major design principles used to represent formality. It is also a principle with which most people are familiar, from their experience with everything from the natural world to manufactured products.

Rhythm, proportion, and emphasis are other design principles that are used to connote formality, but often in more subtle ways than symmetry.

The answer is B.

3. The net-to-gross ratio for a small retail store has been estimated by the architect to be 80%. The client has told the architect that 60,000 ft² (5600 m²) of sales and storage space are required. The architect should plan for a building area of _____ ft² (_____ m²). (Fill in the blank.)

Solution

The net-to-gross ratio is found by dividing the net usable area by the gross area, which includes circulation areas, mechanical rooms, and similar ancillary areas. The desired net usable area is given and the net-to-gross ratio is known, so the needed gross area can be estimated by dividing the net area by the ratio expressed as a decimal.

$$\text{gross area} = \frac{\text{net usable area}}{\text{net-to-gross ratio}}$$

In U.S. units:

$$\text{gross area} = \frac{60{,}000 \text{ ft}^2}{0.80}$$

$$= 75{,}000 \text{ ft}^2$$

In SI units:

$$\text{gross area} = \frac{5600 \text{ m}^2}{0.80}$$

$$= 7000 \text{ m}^2$$

The answer is 75,000 ft² (7000 m²).

4.   Which of the programming diagrams shown would best record required space relationships just prior to initial space planning?

A.

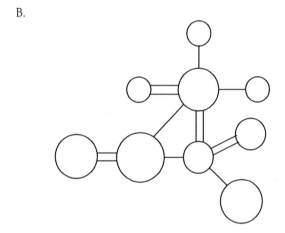

B.

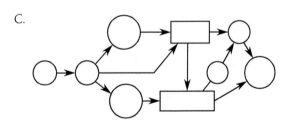

C.

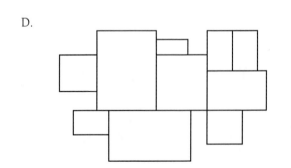

D.

Solution

Option B illustrates a *bubble diagram*. These diagrams are often used to indicate required adjacencies and priorities of relationships. Although it is often derived from the *matrix chart* shown in option A, the bubble diagram is best for showing relationships just prior to space planning, because the relative sizes and positions of the bubbles begin to give an indication of spatial relationships and sizes of the various spaces needed.

Option C is a *flow diagram*, as indicated by the arrows. This would be used as a scheduling chart or to show a flow of materials or some other kind of process from one point to another. Option D shows a *block diagram*, which represents the first results of spatial organization based on an adjacency diagram. It is not the correct answer because the question asks which diagram would be best just *prior* to the start of space planning.

The answer is B.

5.   "A house is a machine for living in," reflects the idea that, like a machine, a house should be functional and serve humans. This expression summarizes the philosophy of

    A.   Marcel Breuer
    B.   Mies van der Rohe
    C.   Le Corbusier
    D.   Buckminster Fuller

Solution

Le Corbusier made this statement to reflect his theory of modernity. Along with many other architects of the time, Le Corbusier distanced himself from the past and based his designs on functionality without ornament so that buildings would be true to their essential purpose. The quotation also implies that design should be efficient, simple, and elegant in a form consistent with function.

The answer is C.

6.   Which of the following is typically NOT part of the project schedule developed by the architect during the programming process?

    A.   architectural services negotiation
    B.   pre-design phase
    C.   bidding time
    D.   construction

Solution

The architect's involvement in scheduling the overall project time frame begins only after the architect is hired, which occurs *after* negotiating for the architect's services.

Study Note: Know the different types of scheduling techniques, such as the Gantt schedule (or bar chart) and the critical path method (CPM).

The answer is A.

7. While developing the preliminary project schedule during the programming phase, which would be the most reliable sources of information about construction time?

I. an annually published cost and scheduling book
II. historical documents on similar projects from the architect's office
III. a contracting firm that has done work for the architect in the past
IV. the construction manager whom the client has hired for the job

    A. I and III only
    B. II and III only
    C. II and IV only
    D. III and IV only

Solution

Records of similar projects that the architect has maintained would be a fairly accurate source of information about the time required to build. From this historical data, the architect could factor in any unique elements of the new project to arrive at a preliminary schedule that would work reasonably well for programming. The best source of current information would be the construction manager who is part of the building team, because that person would have a great deal of experience with managing construction schedules.

Annually published cost and scheduling books would not be a good choice because the scheduling information they contain is typically based on number of hours or manpower required to complete individual aspects of construction. Such books would be more useful for estimating time required to complete components of the overall project. Asking a contractor who previously worked with the architect would not be a good choice because, without assurances that they would be awarded the job, the contractor might not be inclined to give accurate information.

The answer is C.

8. In reviewing a CPM schedule from the contractor, the architect notices that the critical path is 200 calendar days, the total float is 30 days, and the contractor is planning for a 5 day work week. The architect should advise the client that the construction time

    A. will be about 40 weeks
    B. may be as long as 46 weeks
    C. could be shortened to 32 weeks
    D. cannot be delayed more than 6 weeks

Solution

The *critical path* is the sequence of events that must happen as scheduled in order for a project to be completed on time. Dividing 5 work days per calendar week into 200 total days gives a 40-week construction time.

Float represents the range of time during which noncritical activities may start or end without affecting the overall schedule. *Total float* is the individual float times added together, and does not influence the critical path time interval.

The answer is A.

9. Which of the following is a characteristic of a fast-track construction schedule?

    A. The contract for the work is awarded after contractors review the completed construction documents and submit their bids.
    B. The design and construction phases of the project occur simultaneously.
    C. The architect is responsible for scheduling and overseeing the construction process.
    D. The decision to fast-track a project may be postponed until after bids are received.

Solution

In a "fast-tracked" project, the owner, construction manager, contractor, and designer collaborate so that portions of the design and construction phases can occur at the same time. A fast-track schedule can reduce the time of a project from 10% to 30% because it eliminates the bid phase and allows materials with long lead times to be purchased before the building design is completed.

In the traditional design-bid-build process, the architect completes a set of documents to define the scope of the work, and these documents are released to contractors for competitive bidding. In a fast-tracked project, the design documents are developed as construction proceeds and are not final until the project is completed, so option A is false.

Construction sequencing and management of the work are the responsibility of the construction manager or a representative of the general contracting firm, so option C is false. Fast-tracking requires cooperation and coordination among all parties from the start. For this reason, the decision to fast-track must be made at the project's inception, so option D is false.

The answer is B.

10.   The statement "develop a multilevel system of pedestrian circulation" is an example of a

    A. need
    B. programming statement
    C. goal
    D. design concept

Solution

A "multilevel system of pedestrian circulation" implies a definite type of physical solution and describes a *design concept*. This should not be confused with a *programming statement*, which states the problem but does not offer a solution or strategy. A programming statement that might precede the design concept would be something like "separate incompatible circulation functions."

The answer is D.

11.   The developer of a retail shopping complex has estimated through an economic analysis that he can afford to build up to 85,000 ft² (8000 m²) of gross building area. A central, enclosed pedestrian mall will occupy about 6% of the building, and the efficiency ratio is estimated to be 75%. Approximately how much net rentable area will be available?

    A. 59,900 ft² (5640 m²)
    B. 63,700 ft² (6000 m²)
    C. 67,600 ft² (6370 m²)
    D. 107,000 ft² (10 100 m²)

Solution

None of the area of the enclosed mall would be rentable, so subtract the 6% right off the top. Then take 75% of the remainder.

In U.S. units:

$$(85{,}000 \text{ ft}^2)(0.06) = 5100 \text{ ft}^2$$
$$85{,}000 \text{ ft}^2 - 5100 \text{ ft}^2 = 79{,}900 \text{ ft}^2$$
$$(79{,}900 \text{ ft}^2)(0.75) = 59{,}925 \text{ ft}^2$$

In SI units:

$$(8000 \text{ m}^2)(0.06) = 480 \text{ m}^2$$
$$8000 \text{ m}^2 - 480 \text{ m}^2 = 7520 \text{ m}^2$$
$$(7520 \text{ m}^2)(0.75) = 5640 \text{ m}^2$$

The answer is A.

Problems 12 through 14 are based on the following programming situation.

A small medical clinic is being planned for a suburban location on an open, level site. It is to include services of general practice, obstetrics/family planning, testing and laboratories, and dental offices, along with medical offices and an administration area. All together the building will have a net area of about 70,000 ft² (6500 m²). Access to the building is primarily by automobile.

The group developing the project wants the facility to be a comfortable, friendly place that minimizes the anxiety of a visit to the doctor and that makes it as easy as possible to get around. It expects the venture to be successful and each department to grow as the catchment area grows.

12.   In order to meet the goals of the client, which of the following design responses would NOT be appropriate?

    A. Base the size of waiting rooms on a behavior setting where establishing territory should be encouraged.
    B. Group the waiting areas and the reception area together to encourage social interaction.
    C. Develop a different color scheme for each of the separate services.
    D. Arrange individual chair seating against walls and other objects so it faces room entries.

Solution

Grouping the waiting areas and the reception area to encourage interaction would probably be the least desirable option for two reasons. People are usually a little nervous while waiting with strangers and prefer the option to avoid contact in sociofugal space. In addition, because there are different departments in a medium-sized facility, having everyone in one space would be inefficient as well as uncomfortable. One large waiting area would make people feel less at ease and therefore would be counterproductive to the client's goals.

The answer is B.

13. Which of the following organizational concepts would probably be most appropriate for this facility?

    A. grid

    B. axial

    C. central

    D. radial

Solution

Because the facility is expected to grow and because there are several distinct departments, a radial organization would work for the first phase and allow for easy growth. Because the site is ample and flat, terrain would probably not restrict this type of organizational pattern. An axial pattern might work, but because everyone enters in one place for directions and orientation, the central focus of a radial pattern would probably be preferable.

The answer is D.

14. Which of the following aspects of flexibility related to expected growth of the facility is most important in developing the structural framing concept?

    A. convertibility

    B. versatility

    C. expandability

    D. all of the above

Solution

For the first phase of this type of building, most functions would probably be fixed, requiring little need for convertibility in the future or multiple use initially. The primary need of expandability would determine the structural framing system employed so that the building could be added onto easily.

The answer is C.

15. Which of these statements regarding grading is FALSE?

    A. Grading may extend beyond a site's property lines.

    B. Cut and fill should be balanced.

    C. Topsoil should be stripped, saved, and reapplied after rough grading is complete.

    D. Slopes should be graded within their natural angle of repose.

Solution

Grading may not extend beyond a site's property lines. Modified contours must always meet up with existing contours within the boundaries of the site.

The answer is A.

16. A large company is planning to construct new corporate headquarters. The vice president of operations presents a list of personnel, their positions in the firm, and company-mandated space standards to the architect. This list would be described as a

    A. facilities program

    B. functional program

    C. firm program

    D. component program

Solution

A *functional program* provides raw data for analysis and development of a *facilities program*, which considers scope, area requirements, adjacencies, costs, and site analysis. The functional program is usually used to make the case for a new facility by demonstrating that a current facility no longer meets the inhabitants' needs. The owner prepares a functional program (but may be assisted by an architect or programmer) because preparation of this type of program requires an in-depth understanding of the operations of the company.

The answer is B.

17. Which of these is true of a vegetated roof? (Choose the four that apply.)

    A. It reduces the amount of stormwater runoff on a site.

    B. It reduces the impervious surface area on a site.

    C. It increases the amount of water that can be harvested for nonpotable uses such as landscape irrigation and flushing toilets.

    D. It will have a longer lifespan than a conventional membrane roofing system.

    E. It can minimize heat island effects.

    F. It is more expensive to maintain than a traditional roofing system.

Solution

A *vegetated roof* is a roofing system that consists of a layer of plants and soil contained within an impermeable plastic liner on top of the structural roof assembly. Captured rainwater is used to irrigate the plants, and the moisture is released back into the atmosphere through evapotranspiration. Because the rainwater is used for irrigation of the plants on the roof, this technique reduces the amount of water than can be harvested for other nonpotable uses.

A vegetated roof reduces the impervious surface area on a site; as the depth of the pan holding the soil and plants increases, the runoff coefficient of the surface decreases. Garden roofs have the added advantage of minimizing heat island effects. The roofs may be designed as active gardens requiring tending and watering, or may contain plants that require little to no maintenance. Generally, the lifespan of a vegetated roof is longer and overall maintenance costs are less than would be incurred with a conventional roof system because the roofing membrane is protected from ultraviolet radiation by the layers of organic material.

The answer is A, B, D, and E.

18.   A retaining wall is LEAST likely to fail by

   A.   spalling
   B.   sliding
   C.   settling
   D.   overturning

Solution

Retaining walls must resist the force of the soil that they hold back, the wall's weight, and any additional live loads applied. They are most likely to fail in one of three ways.

  • by *sliding*, where the lateral thrust on the wall forces the entire wall to move forward

  • by *settling*, where the vertical force (weight of wall and soil bearing on base) exceeds the bearing capacity of the soil beneath the wall, and the retaining wall sinks

  • by *overturning*, where the overturning moment of the lateral thrust causes the wall to rotate forward. The rotation point is generally the toe of the footing.

Spalling is the deterioration of concrete or masonry caused by excessive moisture and is unlikely to cause a retaining wall to fail.

The answer is A.

19.   The following five activities are completed during the programming phase.

   • collect data
   • define the problem
   • develop programmatic concepts
   • owner describes project goals
   • reconcile list of spaces with project budget

When they are put in the correct order, which will occur third?

   A.   collect data
   B.   define the problem
   C.   develop programmatic concepts
   D.   reconcile list of spaces with project budget

Solution

The correct order of activities is

   • owner describes project goals
   • collect data
   • develop programmatic concepts
   • reconcile list of spaces with project budget
   • define the problem

Programming is a sequence of steps that leads the programmer and owner from a rough idea for a project to a clear statement of the problems and opportunities it presents. These challenges will be considered fully and resolved during the design phase.

To begin programming, it is first necessary to describe the project goals. This step includes a discussion of the owner's objectives for the building, problems that must be addressed, and space requirements.

Next, the programmer collects data. During this phase, the programmer organizes facts regarding the site, the occupants, the intended uses and characteristics of the spaces needed, the budget, and the local codes or ordinances that will affect and influence the project.

During the third step, the programmer develops schematic diagrams in order to organize the facts collected in the previous step and present them in a way that is visually clear and comprehensible. These diagrams, which can take many forms, display the sizes and spatial relationships (adjacencies) of the spaces that are needed or desired.

Next, the programmer must reconcile the list of programmed spaces with the project budget. Now is the time to adjust the program, the budget, or both, so that the project is feasible.

Finally, the programmer defines the problem. This is the goal of programming: to define the problem so that it can be solved during the design phase. What kind of building must be built? How are the spaces within it to be related? Where will it be built? How much will it cost? Programming is the process of seeking problems and defining objectives; design is the process of solving the problems and bringing physical form to those objectives.

The answer is C.

ENVIRONMENTAL, SOCIAL, AND ECONOMIC ISSUES

20. A 50-year-old warehouse that shows no obvious signs of deterioration is to be remodeled as an office building. Which of the following areas should be most carefully evaluated at the start to help determine the project's feasibility? (Choose the four that apply.)

- A. ceiling heights
- B. fire protection systems
- C. foundation
- D. roof
- E. structural framework
- F. windows

Solution

The foundation, roof, structural framework, and windows represent major components of a building. If they are inadequate or in poor condition, they could be too expensive to repair or replace while maintaining project feasibility.

The ceiling heights of a warehouse would be sufficient for an office. Fire protection systems would probably be nonexistent or would have to be upgraded in any event, so this would be less of an initial concern.

The answer is C, D, E, and F.

21. In order to quickly gather and document information for the restoration of a historic building with a large interior dome, the architect should recommend that the client use

- A. field measurements
- B. false-color imaging
- C. photogrammetry
- D. laser scanning

Solution

Laser scanning would be the best choice because this method could quickly make the required remote measurements from just a few points (or possibly even one). Physical access to any part of the dome would not be required.

Photogrammetry would take more time and might require that control points be placed on the dome and hand surveyed to establish a base coordinate system. Standard *field measurements* taken by hand would be very slow, would not be very accurate, and would require extensive scaffolding. *False-color imaging* would not be at all appropriate because this type of analysis provides no information on field measurements.

The answer is D.

22. Prior to commencing schematic design work for the remodeling of a lease space in a strip shopping mall, which of the following types of information would be LEAST important to document?

- A. electrical and telephone outlet locations
- B. bearing wall locations
- C. entry door condition
- D. ceiling condition

Solution

Schematic design work would require good information on existing services, such as telephone and power outlets, the locations of bearing walls for space planning, and whether or not the existing ceiling could be reused. The condition of the entry door is cosmetic and would not be critical for preliminary space planning and schematic design.

The answer is C.

23. In estimating the value of a parcel of land, any of the following approaches may be used EXCEPT the

- A. assessment approach
- B. income approach
- C. market approach
- D. cost approach

Solution

There is no land valuation method known as the assessment approach. *Assessment* is the official valuation of property for the purpose of levying a tax. The other three answers are the various ways assessments can be made initially.

The answer is A.

24. Designing environments so individuals can maintain a comfortable distance between them applies the psychological principles of

    A. territoriality
    B. density
    C. behavior settings
    D. personal space

Solution

The concept of *personal space*, as developed by Edward T. Hall, states that four basic distances can be understood to exist in the study of human behavior, each one appropriate for different private and social situations. These are the intimate distance, the personal distance, the social distance, and the public distance.

> *Study Note:* Review the theories of personal space as described by Edward T. Hall in *The Hidden Dimension* and by Robert Sommer in *Personal Space: The Behavioral Basis of Design.*

Terms to Know

behavior setting: a particular place, with definable boundaries and objects within the place, in which a standing pattern of behavior occurs at a particular time

density: the number of people per unit area

proxemics: a term coined by anthropologist Edward T. Hall and now used to describe the study of the spatial requirements of humans and the effects of population density on behavior, communication, and social interaction

territoriality: a behavioral system in which a person, animal, or group lays claim to an area and defends it against others

The answer is D.

25. Which type of planning concept is represented by Savannah, Georgia?

    A. radial
    B. field
    C. grid
    D. star

Solution

The planning of Savannah is based on a grid system in which wards of 40 houses each are bounded by major streets, with each section of the grid containing a public square.

> *Study Note:* Know the significant planning concepts represented by cities such as Savannah, Georgia; Washington, D.C.; Philadelphia, Pennsylvania; Paris, France; London, England; Letchworth, England; and Welwyn Garden City, England. Familiarity with the planning of medieval cities, the garden city concept, the Cité Industrielle, the City Beautiful movement, and new urbanism is also key.

Significant planners throughout history include Christopher Wren, Georges-Eugène Haussmann, Ebenezer Howard, Tony Garnier, Pierre Charles L'Enfant, Daniel Burnham, Frederick Law Olmstead, Frank Lloyd Wright, and Le Corbusier.

The answer is C.

26. A portion of a recreation area is shown. Which location would be the best site for a restaurant and visitor's center?

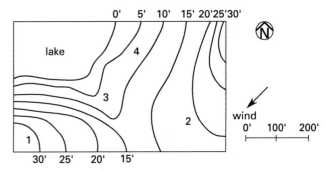

(Multiply ft by 0.305 to obtain m.)

    A. location 1
    B. location 2
    C. location 3
    D. location 4

Solution

Location 1 has a good view, but at the top of a hill it would be very windy. In addition, access to the lake would be difficult due to the steep slope from this site to the water. Location 3 is in a drainage pattern; this alone makes it unsuitable for development, but this area would also be cool due to its position at the bottom of two slopes and in the path of wind coming through the valley. Location 4 has a good view, has easy access to the lake, and could be used for development, but the slightly steeper slope might complicate grading and site work. Location 2 has level ground and a good view of and access to the lake, and its location on a south-facing slope would capture the sun and minimize the detrimental effects of the wind.

The answer is B.

27.   City planning in the United States has been strongly influenced by

I.   the Columbian Exposition of 1893
II.   the Ordinance of 1785
III.   L'Enfant's plan of Washington, DC
IV.   Garnier's *cité industrielle*
V.   the Industrial Revolution

    A.   I, III, and V only
    B.   I, II, and IV only
    C.   I, II, IV, and V only
    D.   I, II, III, IV, and V

Solution

The Columbian Exposition revived interest in city planning and showed that desirable results could be achieved through organized efforts. It also prompted many cities to plan civic centers and parkways. The Ordinance of 1785 started the rectangular survey system, which reinforced the idea of grid planning that began with the plan for Philadelphia. Garnier's plan was developed in response to the Industrial Revolution and was the first to use the idea of zoning. The Industrial Revolution prompted a reform movement that led to many ideas about planning, many of which influenced urban design in Europe and the United States.

Although L'Enfant's plan was widely praised and publicized as a major planning effort, its Baroque planning approach was never widely adopted.

The answer is C.

28.   According to Kevin Lynch's *The Image of the City*, which of the following would probably NOT be considered an element of a city's image?

    A.   a group of houses
    B.   a freeway
    C.   a neighborhood bar
    D.   an area with a high concentration of hospitals

Solution

A freeway can be considered a path, an edge, or both, depending on its function. It is a path to the person traveling on it. It is an edge if it divides a district or encloses an area.

A popular neighborhood gathering spot would probably be considered a node because it can be entered and because it is a center of interest. It would most likely be the center of a neighborhood district as well.

An area with many hospitals would be viewed as the hospital district. This image would be reinforced because of the likely support services, such as doctors' offices and pharmacies, that would also be nearby.

A group of houses by themselves would have little image unless they formed an edge or surrounded a park or similar node.

The answer is A.

29.   Social contact and interaction in a picnic pavilion would be promoted most by

    A.   making the dimensions of the pavilion small enough that the anticipated number of users would cross into each other's "personal distance"
    B.   designing benches around the support columns so people would have a place to sit and talk
    C.   separating the cooking and serving area from the dining area and entrance
    D.   providing a variety of informal spaces of different sizes, locations, and uses

Solution

A variety of informal spaces would promote social contact. Option A is incorrect because forcing too many people within close, personal space would be counterproductive. People would become uncomfortable and defensive. Option B is incorrect because the orientation of the benches would be sociofugal, requiring that people face away from each other. Option C is incorrect because the cooking and serving area would be one of the most popular gathering spaces and a destination for people. Here, people could watch food being prepared, serve themselves, and informally meet other people.

The answer is D.

30. If the contour interval on the map shown is 2 ft (2 m), what is the slope between points A and B?

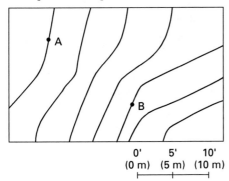

```
0'    5'    10'
(0 m) (5 m) (10 m)
```

- A. 27%
- B. 53%
- C. 67%
- D. not enough information is given to answer

Solution

Using the scale on the drawing, the horizontal distance between the two points is about 15 ft (15 m). The slope is the vertical distance divided by the horizontal distance.

In U.S. units:
$$G = \left(\frac{(4)(2\text{ ft})}{15\text{ ft}}\right) \times 100\% = 53\%$$

In SI units:
$$G = \left(\frac{(4)(2\text{ m})}{15\text{ m}}\right) \times 100\% = 53\%$$

The answer is B.

31. A speculative office building probably would not be built if the developer discovered that

- A. all of the catchment area was not served by arterial streets
- B. the site consisted of mostly sandy soil with a 6 ft (1.8 m) top layer of expansive clay
- C. the vacancy rate of office space in the city was three times the national average
- D. the neighborhood community objected to the sight of parking lots

Solution

The vacancy rate in the region or community is the one factor that would most affect the financial success of the project and the decision to build.

A speculative office building depends on a wide catchment area, and a lack of arterial roads in some portions of it

would most likely not affect the marketability of the project. If there was strong objection to parking lots, the visual impact could be minimized through landscaping, or parking could be placed underground or in a well-designed parking structure.

Option B is incorrect because either a relatively thin layer of clay only 6 ft (1.8 m) thick could be removed and replaced with better soil, or the foundations could be placed on the good underlying layer of sandy soil.

The answer is C.

32. Which of the following is a frequent cause of foundation problems?

- A. extensive underground rock formations just below the surface
- B. a 5 ft (1.5 m) water table
- C. expansive clay and organic soil
- D. all of the above

Solution

All the conditions listed would create unusual excavation and foundation problems.

The answer is D.

33. Which of the automobile entrances to the site shown is most desirable?

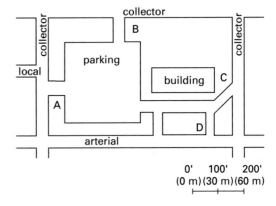

```
0'   100'  200'
(0 m)(30 m)(60 m)
```

- A. entrance A
- B. entrance B
- C. entrance C
- D. entrance D

Solution

The most desirable entrance location is the one located in the collector street, Entrance B. Entrance A is too close to another intersecting street. Entrance C intersects the street at an angle that is unsafe. Entrance D intersects an arterial street. Although sometimes possible, this situation should be avoided, especially if it is as close to an intersection as is this one.

The answer is B.

34. Which of the following contour line signatures represents a ridge?

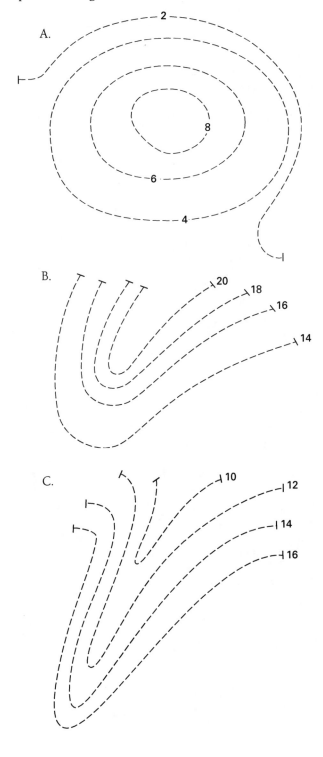

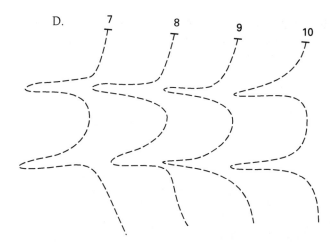

Solution

Contours are used to represent three-dimensional land-forms in a two-dimensional drawing. Ridges and valleys are frequently confused; the contours point toward the lower elevation for a ridge and toward the higher elevation for a valley.

Hills are generally easy to spot as they are represented with concentric circles (or near circles), but the elevations must be checked to determine whether the landform is a hill or a depression. The elevations near the center are higher for a hill and lower for a depression.

Contours with very regular spacing usually represent some human-made element on the site, such as a street with a curb and gutter.

The answer is B.

35. The intellectual, cultural, and artistic culture of a time and place is known as

    A. an epoch
    B. a zeitgeist
    C. an era
    D. a movement

Solution

The intellectual, cultural, and artistic culture of a time and place is known as its *zeitgeist* (sometimes the term is capitalized). Zeitgeist is a German word that means "the spirit of the time." It is particularly relevant in discussions of art and architecture, as both are evidence of the philosophies and values of the people who created them. Many periods in architectural history, including the Arts and Crafts movement, the Bauhaus, Expressionism, and so on, sprang from philosophical theory.

The answer is B.

36. Which parking configuration is most difficult for a driver to maneuver within?

- A. 90°
- B. 60°
- C. 45°
- D. 30°

Solution

The most difficult parking configuration for a driver to maneuver within is a 90° angle arrangement. This is the only parking configuration listed that allows a two-way travel lane, and it is the most efficient of the four choices, allowing about 11 cars to park for each 100 lineal ft (30.5 m) of curb. However, as a driver is pulling in or backing out of the space, he or she must be aware of traffic coming from either direction, and drivers must make a 90° turn into the parking space.

Both 45° angle and 60° angle configurations are relatively economical and allow easy access to and from parking spaces. They permit only one-way traffic aisles. A 45° angle configuration will allow approximately eight cars to park for each 100 lineal ft (30.5 m) of curb. A 60° angle configuration allows about nine cars to park for each 100 lineal ft (30.5 m) of curb.

30° angle configurations are the least efficient, allowing only about 5 cars to park within each 100 lineal ft (30.5 m) of curb. They permit only a one-way traffic lane, and are seldom used because they are uneconomical.

The answer is A.

37. During preservation of an 1880s farmhouse that was the childhood home of a prominent state governor, the owners discover that termites have attacked the large wooden beam supporting the first floor. The damage is particularly bad at the ends of the beam, where the beam rests in pockets in the masonry foundation walls. Which of the following repairs would be the best choice in this situation?

- A. Support the beam with a row of metal columns.
- B. Remove the beam and replace it with a steel or laminated wood member sized to adequately carry the floor loads.
- C. Drill through the beam, insert reinforcing, and fill the voids with injectable epoxy.
- D. Sister additional structural members to the beam.

Solution

The key word in this question is *preservation*. A preservation project dictates that the least amount possible be done to stabilize a building and that any interventions be made as invisibly as possible. The best (although not necessarily most economical) choice for repairing this beam would be to drill through the solid part of the wood into the damaged area, insert reinforcing (usually a plastic rod), and then inject epoxy resin through the drilled holes. The resin will fill the termite-damaged areas as well as the drilled holes and bind to the wood. This process is known to preservationists as *consolidation*. The repair will meet or exceed the original strength of the member, and the resin can be sanded and finished to match the surrounding wood.

The answer is C.

38. One of the hallmarks of the plan developed by Clarence Stein and Henry Wright in 1928 for the town of Radburn, New Jersey, was the use of underpasses to allow pedestrian traffic to pass under automobile traffic. This was intended to prevent accidents and keep pedestrian paths separate from vehicular paths. Which other "new town" features this separation of pedestrian and vehicular traffic?

- A. Beverly Hills, California
- B. Seaside, Florida
- C. Reston, Virginia
- D. Chestnut Hill, Pennsylvania

Solution

The plan for Radburn, New Jersey, developed by Stein and Wright in 1928, was one of the first to take on the challenge of planning for both pedestrians and drivers. Although only one underpass was actually constructed in Radburn, the concept of underpasses for pedestrian traffic is still associated with this plan. Stein and Wright attributed the idea for the underpasses to Frederick Law Olmstead and Calvert Vaux, who utilized changes in grade to separate greenspace from traffic paths in Central Park in New York City. Reston, Virginia, features a series of underpasses that promote travel on foot throughout the community.

The answer is C.

39. Which of the following cities was the first in the United States to establish a "historic district" to preserve endangered properties?

    A. Williamsburg, Virginia
    B. Savannah, Georgia
    C. New Orleans, Louisiana
    D. Charleston, South Carolina

Solution

Charleston, South Carolina, invented the concept of the "historic district" in 1931 as a response to attrition of its aging building stock through theft, demolition, and neglect. The historic district designation was added to the zoning ordinance to make it legally enforceable, and an architectural review board was established to review plans for all work within the historic area.

New Orleans designated the Vieux Carré a historic district in 1937, adopting the mechanisms instituted in Charleston. In the late 1920s and early 1930s, part of Williamsburg, Virginia, was acquired and restored, preserved, or reconstructed by what is now the Colonial Williamsburg Foundation, led by Reverend W.A.R. Goodwin and financed by John D. Rockefeller. After the restoration, the city of Williamsburg designated areas surrounding the historic area as architectural review districts and the city now requires that modifications and new construction be approved by the architectural review board. In the 1960s, the people of Savannah began revival of the Pulaski Ward.

The answer is D.

40. Which of the following statements about Gothic architecture is FALSE?

    A. The use of flying buttresses made possible more fenestration in the nave walls.
    B. A Gothic arch exerts less thrust than a rounded arch spanning the same distance.
    C. By necessity, the plan of a Gothic cathedral was always based on a square bay.
    D. A ribbed vault is comprised of three pairs of arches per bay.

Solution

Gothic architecture rose to prominence in the 1100s through 1300s and was a popular style of building for religious structures. Well-known examples include Amiens Cathedral, the Abbey Church of St. Denis, Notre Dame, the Chartes Cathedral, and the Reims Cathedral, all in France, and the Canterbury Cathedral, St. Albans Cathedral, and Salisbury Cathedral, all in England. Buildings in the Gothic style were also constructed late in this period in Spain and Germany.

The most easily recognizable feature of Gothic architecture is the pointed arch. This new form made it possible to construct a vault with a lighter structural shell than was possible using semicircular arches. A pointed arch exerts less thrust than a rounded arch of similar size.

In Gothic architecture, the thrust of the arches was counteracted by massive flying buttresses constructed on the exteriors of buildings. These buttresses allowed the exterior walls to be thinner and made possible larger amounts of tracery and fenestration than previous construction methods had.

A ribbed vault is comprised of three pairs of arches oriented diagonally, transversely, and longitudinally; the space between the arches is filled in with a thin shell of stone.

While the semicircular arch worked well only with square plan forms, the pointed arch allowed vaults to be constructed over bays that were square, rectangular, or oddly shaped.

The answer is C.

CODES AND REGULATIONS

41. Spray-on fireproofing containing asbestos was banned from use in building construction in

    A. 1968
    B. 1973
    C. 1980
    D. 1989

Solution

The Environmental Protection Agency (EPA) banned the spray application of asbestos-containing fireproofing materials in 1973.

The answer is B.

42. In the renovation of a historic structure, the treatment approach that attempts to retain the most historic materials and spaces while allowing replacement of damaged exterior materials is

    A. preservation
    B. rehabilitation
    C. restoration
    D. reconstruction

Solution

Rehabilitation emphasizes the retention and repair of historic materials but gives some latitude for replacement of damaged materials. This is one of the four basic types of treatments that can be applied to historic structures.

    Study Note: Know the differences among the terms *preservation* (the most historically accurate), *rehabilitation*, *restoration*, and *reconstruction* (the least historically accurate).

The answer is B.

43. A client wants to obtain federal tax credits for rehabilitation of an old building that has been designated as a state historic landmark. The architect should inform the client that

    A. new additions or exterior alterations cannot vary from the historic character
    B. a thorough historic survey is required to verify conformity to federal standards
    C. the Secretary of the Interior's Standards for Rehabilitation must be met
    D. the cost might exceed the client's budget because state standards must be used

Solution

The Standards for Rehabilitation (often called the Secretary of the Interior's Standards for Rehabilitation) developed by the Heritage Preservation Services branch of the National Park Service must be met if federal investment tax credits are to be used. These standards take precedence over any state or local requirements.

Option A is incorrect because the standards do allow for new additions and alterations to be differentiated from the old while still being compatible in massing, size, scale, and architectural features. Option B is incorrect because a survey and study of the subject property in itself does not guarantee conformance with the federal standards. Option D is incorrect because a cost higher than the budget is not related to the ability to receive a federal tax credit.

The answer is C.

44. According to the United States Survey system, a section of land is a square shape. The dimension along the sides of the square is most nearly

    A. 0.5 mi
    B. 1 mi
    C. 6 mi
    D. 24 mi

Solution

A *section* is a 1 mi square parcel of land containing 640 ac.

A *check* is an area 24 mi on a side bounded by parallels and meridians. A *township* is 6 mi on a side. A *quarter section* is 0.5 mi on a side.

    Study Note: The United States Survey system, begun in 1784, divided U.S. land that was not already surveyed into a square grid system of meridians 24 mi apart. These squares are called checks. Each check is divided into 16 townships, each 6 mi on a side. Each township is further divided into 36 1 mi wide sections of land. The sections are further divided into quarter sections, and each quarter section is then quartered.

Be aware that an acre of land is equal to 43,560 ft². (One hectare of land is equal to 10 000 m².)

Terms to Know

baseline: a parallel used as a primary starting point for the east-west layout of the U.S. survey system

guide meridian: a meridian between the principal meridians

meridian: north-south lines that follow the longitudes of the earth and that are used as the basis for the U.S. survey system

metes-and-bounds property description: a verbal description of land that begins at a known point and describes the bearing and length of each side of the property, in turn, until the point of beginning is reached

parallels: east-west lines that follow the latitudes of the earth

principal meridian: a meridian that serves as the basis for the north-south grid layout of the U.S. survey system

range: the row of townships running north and south from a principal meridian, given a number to describe where it is located north and south of a baseline

standard parallels: parallels between the baselines in the U.S. survey system

township: the row of townships running east and west from a baseline, given a number to describe where it is located east or west of a principal meridian

The answer is B.

45. An architect is asked to calculate the rentable area of the following office space according to ANSI/BOMA Z65.1, *Office Buildings: Standard Methods of Measurement*. The columns are 1 ft by 1 ft (305 by 305). The exterior walls are 1 ft (305) thick and the inside face of the glass is 6 in (152) from the inside face of the interior wall. The corridor walls and demising walls are 4 in (102) thick. Which of the following statements is NOT correct?

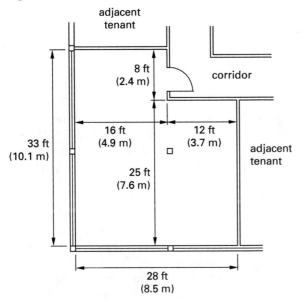

A. The width of the office is 28 ft 8 in (8.7 m).
B. The length of the office is 33 ft (10.1 m).
C. The area occupied by the column would be included in the rentable area.
D. The rentable area would include a share of common restrooms and corridors.

Solution

Calculations of the rentable area of an office follow different rules from calculations of the architectural area of a space. To calculate the rentable area of a space, use the following guidelines.

- When measuring from an exterior wall in which more than 50% of the wall is glass, measure from the inside face of the glass.

- Measure to the inside face of walls between the office and the corridor.

- Measure to the centerline of *demising walls*, or walls between tenants.

- The rentable area would also include a share of common restrooms and corridors.

- No deductions are made for columns or projections necessary to the building.

The answer is B.

46. The distance from the most remote point in a building to the nearest exit is called the

A. common path of egress travel
B. length of exit discharge travel
C. exit separation distance
D. exit access travel distance

Solution

The *exit access travel distance* is the distance a building occupant must travel from the most remote point in the occupied portion of the exit access to the entrance of the nearest exit.

The *common path of egress travel* is that portion of an exit access that the occupants are required to traverse before two separate and distinct paths of egress travel to two exits are available. Option B is incorrect because there is no such thing as length of exit discharge travel. Option C is incorrect because *exit separation distance* refers to the minimum distance by which two exits must be separated when two exits are required.

> *Study Note:* Review the *International Building Code* for exiting nomenclature and definitions related to egress.

The answer is D.

47. The owner of the lot shown wants to develop a building with the maximum allowable gross square footage.

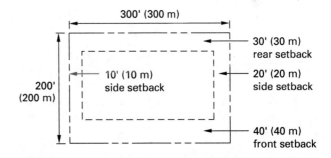

If the floor area ratio (FAR) is 2.0 and the owner builds only full stories to the setback lines, how high will the building be?

A. two stories
B. three stories
C. four stories
D. five stories

Solution

The area of the lot is 60,000 ft² (60,000 m²). If the floor area ratio is 2, the maximum amount of floor area that can be built is 120,000 ft² (120,000 m²). The available ground area that can be covered within the setbacks is 270 ft times 130 ft, or 35,100 ft² (270 m times 130 m, or 35,100 m²). Dividing this figure into 120,000 gives 3.42 stories, which indicates that three full stories can be built.

The answer is B.

48.   The process of strategic facility planning begins with the analysis of three basic business drivers. What are they? (Choose the three that apply.)

    A.   the company's geographic location
    B.   the company's overall sales
    C.   the company's revenue
    D.   local business regulations
    E.   market volatility
    F.   the number of employees in the company

Solution

Strategic facility planning is a niche service that some architectural firms offer. These firms have expanded the traditional definition of architectural programming to include market analysis and business planning for their clients. Architects who offer this specialty often team with professionals in allied fields such as business, law, industrial engineering, or real estate to offer a comprehensive package of services.

The process of strategic facility planning begins with the analysis of business drivers. Three basic business drivers are considered: the company's revenue, its number of employees, and its overall sales. These data give the analysts a sense of where the company stands in relationship to its competitors.

The team then considers the type and goals of the organization. Corporate clients have a different approach to decision making than nonprofit and government sector clients, and the issues of greatest importance to each must be understood before a particular client can be advised. Demand-side factors (those that benefit the end user) and supply-side factors (those that benefit the landlord) are weighed as well. Depending on the client, these factors may or may not include geographic location, local business regulations, and market volatility. Finally, all these factors are considered in the development of a plan for space utilization and possible growth.

The answer is B, C, and F.

49.   Which of these can zoning ordinances do? (Choose the four that apply.)

    A.   influence building form
    B.   determine the allowable flooring loading based on occupancy
    C.   stabilize property values
    D.   determine required amounts of parking
    E.   allow city governments to predict infrastructure needs
    F.   establish the required number of toilet facilities at a municipal stadium

Solution

Zoning ordinances are enacted in municipalities to control what types of structures are built in certain locations. Zoning requirements such as setbacks, floor area ratios, and height limitations influence the form of the building that can be constructed on a site and consequently influence the appearance of a neighborhood. Zoning regulations prohibit construction of incongruent building types within a specific area; for example, zoning ordinances would likely separate residential neighborhoods from heavy industrial uses, helping to stabilize property values. Zoning also helps governments plan for the future by restricting the capacity of the land and helping predict the types and capacities of utility systems necessary in a specific area.

The answer is A, C, D, and E.

50.   Which of the following are required components of an incentive zoning plan?

I.   base floor area ratio
II.   floor area ratio cap
III.   bonus ratio
IV.   bonus cap

    A.   I and II
    B.   I and III
    C.   II and III
    D.   I, II, III, and IV

Solution

Incentive zoning is a way to encourage private developers to provide amenities for public use in exchange for the opportunity to build a larger or taller structure on a site. An example of incentive zoning is the bonus floor area given to developers of New York City skyscrapers who include a public plaza on the ground floor level.

Incentive zoning plans must include a *base floor area ratio* (the standard against which to compare) and a *bonus ratio*—the floor area ratio (FAR) that is provided if the public space is a part of the design. The plans may include caps on the FAR and the bonus FAR—for example, a bonus may be given for providing public parking in an underground garage to increase from the base FAR of 1.5, but the bonus FAR may not exceed 2. For incentive zoning to truly be an incentive, the value of the additional (leasable) floor area must exceed the cost of providing the public amenity.

The answer is B.

51. According to the *ADA/ABA Guidelines*, what is the minimum width of an accessible parking space?

    A.   96 in (2440)
    B.   102 in (2590)
    C.   108 in (2745)
    D.   120 in (3050)

Solution

Accessible parking spaces must be a minimum of 96 in, or 8 ft (2440), wide. An access alley at least 60 in (1525) wide for cars and at least 96 in (2440) wide for vans must be provided adjacent to the space.

The answer is A.

52. A three-story speculative office building has a footprint of 6724 ft² (625 m²). The floors are equal in size. The building is sited on a 1.5 ac (0.61 ha) parcel. The floor area ratio is approximately

    A.   0.1:1
    B.   0.3:1
    C.   0.6:1
    D.   1:1

Solution

The *floor area ratio* expresses the relationship between the square footage of the building and the area of the site on which it is constructed. Zoning ordinances often set limits on the maximum floor area ratio allowed within a region as a means of controlling development density.

In U.S. units:

$$\text{FAR} = \frac{\text{total building area}}{\text{total site area}}$$

$$= \frac{(3 \text{ floors})\left(6724 \, \frac{\text{ft}^2}{\text{floor}}\right)}{(1.5 \text{ ac})\left(43{,}560 \, \frac{\text{ft}^2}{\text{ac}}\right)}$$

$$= 0.31 \quad (0.3{:}1)$$

In SI units:

$$\text{FAR} = \frac{\text{total building area}}{\text{total site area}}$$

$$= \frac{(3 \text{ floors})\left(625 \, \frac{\text{m}^2}{\text{floor}}\right)}{(0.61 \text{ ha})\left(10\,000 \, \frac{\text{m}^2}{\text{ha}}\right)}$$

$$= 0.31 \quad (0.3{:}1)$$

The answer is B.

53. Which of the following would NOT be included in a zoning ordinance?

    A.   maximum building heights
    B.   minimum parking requirements
    C.   maximum numbers of occupants
    D.   minimum setbacks from property lines

Solution

A *zoning ordinance* is a set of rules enacted by a local governing body or by a board that the governing body has designated, such as a zoning or planning commission. This set of rules regulates the types of building and development that are permitted in certain areas of a jurisdiction.

Zoning ordinances specify what uses are permitted in certain areas and may separate the land within the jurisdiction into commercial, industrial, and residential zones. In addition, zoning ordinances typically dictate how a site may be developed, by establishing floor area ratios, minimum lot sizes and dimensions, maximum lot coverage requirements, maximum building heights, minimum setbacks from property lines, and parking requirements.

Sometimes a zoning ordinance gives different requirements from the building code in effect in the same region. This often happens, for example, with requirements for maximum height and area. Building codes determine these maximums on the basis of occupancy groups and types of

18 PROGRAMMING, PLANNING & PRACTICE

construction, modified by factors such as whether the building will be sprinklered and whether access for fire-fighting equipment will be provided. If the local zoning ordinance and the building code give different maximum heights or areas, the lower of the two takes precedence.

A zoning ordinance would not determine the maximum number of occupants permitted in a structure. This requirement is established by the building code in the jurisdiction, in accordance with the occupancy group and type of construction of the building.

The answer is C.

54.   Each area listed below is included in the plans for the construction of a new high school. Which areas do NOT have to comply with the *ADA/ABA Guidelines*? (Choose the four that apply.)

    A.   copy room designated "faculty only"

    B.   lifeguard tower within the indoor pool area

    C.   catwalks for auditorium lighting

    D.   contractor's on-site construction trailer

    E.   temporary passageway during construction for pedestrian access to the football field

    F.   referee stand at a volleyball game

Solution

The *ADA/ABA Guidelines* state that all newly designed or newly constructed areas must meet accessibility requirements. This includes all employee work areas and all temporary construction that is open to the public (such as a protected walkway, temporary seating for a special event, and so forth).

The following areas are not required to be accessible.

- temporary facilities associated with the process of construction (job site trailer, scaffolding)

- raised areas used primarily for security or life safety (lifeguard tower, security guard tower)

- non-occupiable service areas accessed infrequently for maintenance or monitoring (catwalks, penthouses, pump rooms)

- single occupant structures accessed from above or below grade (such as a tollbooth accessed through an underground tunnel)

- raised structures for officiating sporting events

- water slides

- nonpublic animal containment areas

- raised boxing and wrestling rings

The answer is B, C, D, and F.

55.   Which of the following areas may exits pass through? (Choose all that apply.)

    A.   office reception areas

    B.   building lobbies

    C.   unoccupied storage areas

    D.   apartment entries

    E.   kitchens

    F.   stairwells

Solution

The *International Building Code* specifically states that exits cannot pass through kitchens; through storerooms, closets, or other spaces used for similar purposes; or through rooms that can be locked to prevent egress. Lobbies, reception areas, entries, and stairwells may all be parts of the path of egress. However, to be part of an exit, a space is not permitted to be locked from the inside under any circumstances.

The answer is A, B, D, and F.

56.   An architect is planning a 30 ft by 35 ft addition to a community library. The entire addition will be a single large meeting room. This room will be used for "story hour" and other library programs, and will also be made available to community organizations for meetings and presentations. The space will be open with no fixed seating. Using the information in the table shown, what is the maximum occupancy of this space?

function of space	floor area per occupant (ft²)
assembly without fixed seats	
concentrated (chairs only—not fixed)	7 net
standing space	5 net
unconcentrated (tables and chairs)	15 net
business area	100 gross
library	
reading room	50 net
stack area	100 gross

(Multiply ft² by 0.093 to obtain m².)

Adapted from Table 1004.1.1, Maximum Floor Area Allowances per Occupant, 2009 International Building Code.

    A.   30 occupants

    B.   70 occupants

    C.   150 occupants

    D.   210 occupants

PPI • www.ppi2pass.com

Solution

A library or community hall is classified as an A-3 (Assembly) occupancy according to the *International Building Code* (IBC). If fixed seating is provided, the number of occupants equals the number of seats. Where no fixed seating is provided, the designer must refer to IBC Table 1004.1.1 to calculate the occupancy of a space.

The maximum occupancy of the space is the greatest possible number of occupants as calculated using the IBC table. If tables and chairs are provided, each occupant is allocated 15 ft² (1.4 m²). If the room will be arranged with rows of seating, each person occupies 7 ft² (0.7 m²). If occupants are standing, each is allocated 5 ft² (0.5 m²) of standing space.

The usage that allocates the least space per occupant will give the greatest occupancy, so dividing the area of the room by 5 ft² (0.5 m²) gives in the maximum occupancy of this space.

In U.S. units:

$$(30 \text{ ft})(35 \text{ ft}) = 1050 \text{ ft}^2$$

$$\frac{1050 \text{ ft}^2}{5 \dfrac{\text{ft}^2}{\text{occupant}}} = 210 \text{ occupants}$$

In SI units:

$$(9 \text{ m})(11 \text{ m}) = 99 \text{ m}^2$$

$$\frac{99 \text{ m}^2}{0.47 \dfrac{\text{m}^2}{\text{occupant}}} = 210 \text{ occupants}$$

The answer is D.

57. A new restaurant has a maximum occupancy of 300 people. For all exits, the building code requires an allowance of 0.2 in (5) per occupant. Calculate the minimum number and size of exits.

    A. one exit, 5 ft 0 in (1524) pair of doors
    B. one exit, 6 ft 0 in (1829) pair of doors
    C. two exits, two 30 in (762) doors
    D. two exits, two 3 ft 0 in (914) doors

Solution

Because there are more than 50 occupants in this space, two exits must be provided. These exits must be separate and a certain minimum distance apart so that a fire is unlikely to block both. To calculate the minimum size of the required exits from the space, multiply the maximum number of occupants by 0.2 in (5) per occupant.

In U.S. units:

$$(300 \text{ occupants})\left(0.2 \frac{\text{in}}{\text{occupant}}\right) = 60 \text{ in}$$

In SI units:

$$(300 \text{ occupants})\left(5 \frac{\text{mm}}{\text{occupant}}\right) = 1500 \text{ mm}$$

Because two exits must be provided, the minimum width per exit would be 30 in (762). However, accessibility standards and component requirements both call for a minimum clear opening width of 32 in (813) for each door. This width is generally achieved by using a 36 in (914) door. Therefore, the best answer is two exits, two 3 ft 0 in (914) doors.

The answer is D.

58. The abbreviated table shown includes requirements for occupancy loads. A restaurant on the ground floor contains 3500 ft² (326 m²) of dining area, a 1000 ft² (93 m²) kitchen, and a 1200 ft² (112 m²) bar area. What is the total occupant load?

use	occupant load factor (ft²/occupant)
assembly areas, concentrated use (without fixed seats)	7
auditoriums	
dance floors	
lodge rooms	
assembly areas, less-concentrated use	15
conference rooms	
dining rooms	
drinking establishments	
exhibit rooms	
lounges	
stages	
hotels and apartments	200
kitchens—commercial	200
offices	100
stores, ground floor	30

(Multiply ft² by 0.093 to obtain m².)

    A. 202 occupants
    B. 318 occupants
    C. 380 occupants
    D. 409 occupants

Solution

From the table, assembly areas, including restaurants and bars, have an occupant load of 15. Commercial kitchens have an occupant load of 200. Therefore,

In U.S. units:

$$\text{dining area} = \frac{3500 \text{ ft}^2}{15 \dfrac{\text{ft}^2}{\text{occupant}}} = 233 \text{ occupants}$$

$$\text{kitchen} = \frac{1000 \text{ ft}^2}{200 \dfrac{\text{ft}^2}{\text{occupant}}} = 5 \text{ occupants}$$

$$\text{bar} = \frac{1200 \text{ ft}^2}{15 \dfrac{\text{ft}^2}{\text{occupant}}} = 80 \text{ occupants}$$

$$\text{total} = 318 \text{ occupants}$$

In SI units:

$$\text{dining area} = \frac{326 \text{ m}^2}{1.4 \dfrac{\text{m}^2}{\text{occupant}}} = 233 \text{ occupants}$$

$$\text{kitchen} = \frac{93 \text{ m}^2}{19 \dfrac{\text{m}^2}{\text{occupant}}} = 5 \text{ occupants}$$

$$\text{bar} = \frac{112 \text{ m}^2}{1.4 \dfrac{\text{m}^2}{\text{occupant}}} = 80 \text{ occupants}$$

$$\text{total} = 318 \text{ occupants}$$

The answer is B.

59.   Under the *International Building Code*, which of the following are correct statements?

I.   Fire zone 3 is the most restrictive.
II.   Required fire resistance of exterior, nonbearing walls is determined by type of construction, occupancy, and distance from property lines.
III. Exit doors must swing in the direction of travel.
IV.   The legal basis for building codes in the United States is the U.S. Constitution.
V.   Occupant load is independent of occupancy group.

    A.   I, III, and IV only
    B.   II, III, and V only
    C.   II, IV, and V only
    D.   I, II, IV, and V only

Solution

Fire zone 1, not 3, is the most restrictive. Exit doors must swing in the direction of travel only when the occupant load is greater than 50.

The other three statements are true. Occupant load is dependent only on the uses given in IBC Table 1004.1.1 and the various factors based on net or gross floor area.

The answer is C.

PROJECT AND PRACTICE MANAGEMENT

60. The type of foundation system to be used on a construction project should be determined by

    A.   the structural engineer
    B.   a geotechnical engineer
    C.   a civil engineer
    D.   the architect

Solution

The geotechnical engineer makes the various soil tests required for a particular site and suggests the type of foundation, based on the bearing capacity of the soil and other factors. However, responsibilty for the design of the foundation and type of system employed is ultimately the structural engineer's.

Typically, the geotechnical engineer's report is contracted and paid for by the client, and the services of the structural engineer are included in the architect's scope of services.

The answer is A.

61.   In order to finance public improvements with the goal of encouraging private development, a city's redevelopment agency would most likely use

    A.   general obligation bonds
    B.   developer impact fees
    C.   business improvement districts
    D.   tax increment financing

Solution

Tax increment financing is a method cities use to issue bonds to pay for improvements (such as new sewers or streets) within a specified district that are intended to stimulate private development within the district. During the time of redevelopment, taxes are based on the assessed valuation prior to the redevelopment. After the development period, the increase in taxes due to the development (the tax increment) is used to repay the bonds.

General obligation bonds are typically used to fund a specific project, such as a library or fire station. They are not used to encourage private development, although later private development could be a consequence of the new public facility being constructed (such as apartments or restaurants built in the vicinity of a publicly funded baseball stadium). Because all taxpayers in the jurisdiction issuing the general obligation bonds must pay off the bonds through a property tax, a voter majority is required.

Developer impact fees are generally used to fund infrastructure improvements made necessary by new development. Although these fees are a common method of raising money, they can have a negative effect because developers look for areas to build in where impact fees are not charged.

Business improvement districts are used to fund public space improvements, such as streetscapes, to enhance an area's appeal and, indirectly, its property values. Taxes are assessed on those property owners in the district who would benefit from the improvements, so this type of financing is not intended to encourage private development.

Terms to Know

ad valorem tax: a tax based on the value of the property being taxed

The answer is D.

---

62. A client has requested that the time for design and construction document production be shortened. The architect's best course of action would be to

- A. hire additional employees
- B. have the design team work overtime
- C. assign more existing employees to the design team
- D. ask the client to reduce the scope of the project

Solution

Of the options given, trying to utilize existing employees would make the most sense from the standpoint of personnel and office management.

Hiring new employees would be shortsighted unless their long-term need was assured. Having people work overtime is generally not an efficient or productive approach in the long run and should not be used to complete an entire project. The client should not have to reduce the scope of the

project just to accommodate the lack of staffing in the architect's office. The architect may be justified in asking for a change to the owner-architect agreement if the original project parameters are changed by the client.

The answer is C.

---

63. Which of the following is normally NOT provided as part of an architect's standard services?

- A. a project manual
- B. program development services
- C. structural design services
- D. a review of shop drawings

Solution

Under Article 5 of AIA Document B101, *Standard Form of Agreement Between Owner and Architect*, the owner is responsible for furnishing a program setting forth the owner's objectives, schedule, and space requirements and relationships. However, at the time of writing the agreement between architect and owner, the architect and owner may mutually designate additional services. These additional services are listed in a table in Article 4. If the client requests programming development or other services not normally performed, they should be listed here.

> *Study Note:* Normally, the owner is also required to furnish a property survey and the services of geotechnical engineers (soils reports).

The answer is B.

---

64. An architect has been asked to develop an agreement for services between owner and architect to design a small, speculative office building for a new client. In order to increase the likelihood of making a profit on the project, what method of determining compensation should the architect propose?

- A. rate per square foot (square meter)
- B. stipulated sum
- C. percentage of the work
- D. multiple of direct personnel expense

Solution

The *multiple of direct personnel expense* includes the salaries of people working on the job and their required benefits, plus overhead and profit. Because this is a time-based method of compensation, each hour spent working on the project includes a profit factor. For a new client wanting a speculative type of building, the architect should use the multiple of direct personnel expense method, to increase the odds of getting paid for all services performed.

There are too many unknowns to use the other compensation methods. Methods based on *area* are best used for repetitive types of projects for which the architect has good historical time and expense data. Work based on a *stipulated sum* may run over the originally allotted time, decreasing or eliminating any profit first estimated. With a *percentage of the work* method, a great deal of time may be expended even on a low-cost building, such as a speculative office.

> *Study Note:* There are at least 10 methods of calculating compensation for architectural services. Four are time-based: multiple of direct salary expense, multiple of direct personnel expense, professional fee plus expenses, and hourly billing rate. Other methods include stipulated sum, percentage of cost of the work, square footage, unit cost, multiple of consultants' billings, and royalty. In many cases, different methods of compensation are combined on the same project.

The answer is D.

65. Which of the following project management activities would most likely ensure that construction documents are completed on schedule and within budget?

    A. documenting all meetings and correspondence
    B. establishing time and fee projections
    C. monitoring time sheets
    D. setting milestones

Solution

Monitoring the progress of a job is critical to ensuring that the original schedule and fee projects are being met.

Although establishing time and fee projections is a critical component of project management early in the project, continual monitoring is also required. Setting milestones for when certain intermediate work is to be completed is also important, but actual work completion must be compared with the estimated schedule to meet the final deadline.

The answer is C.

66. When deciding whether to accept a project from a potential client, the architect should be most concerned with the

    A. architect's current level of staffing
    B. project's financial feasibility
    C. project's distance from the architect's office
    D. question of whether the client has worked with an architect before

Solution

Although the architect should be concerned with all of the parameters listed, the financial feasibility of the project is the most important. Without a viable project, the architect may perform preliminary work without getting paid, and the project might never be completed.

The answer is B.

67. When developing a schedule for design services, the architect should be concerned about all of the following EXCEPT the

    A. architect's number of available staff
    B. client's decision-making and approval process
    C. structural consultant's workload
    D. size of the project

Solution

The architect does not have direct control over the consultants' workload or ability to do any given job.

The design schedule is impacted by the size and complexity of the project, the number of people available to work on the project, and how quickly the client can make required decisions and approve the architect's work during the various stages of the design. In addition, the abilities and design methodology of the architect's team can affect the time it takes to produce a job.

The answer is C.

68. An electrical engineer would typically perform load calculations and develop panel schedules in which phase of basic services?

    A. pre-design
    B. schematic design
    C. design development
    D. construction documents

Solution

Prior to doing load calculations and developing the specific panel schedules, the electrical engineer would need specific information from the architect concerning power outlet locations and service needs of the equipment the client was planning on using. This information would be developed during the pre-design (programming), schematic design, and design development phases and would then be available to the electrical engineer for design development. The final checking and drafting would be done during the construction documents phase.

Study Note: Know the responsibilities of the various consultants during the major design phases of a project.

The answer is C.

69. During a construction project, the electrical contractor discovers a code violation error on the electrical engineer's drawings. Determining how to correct the problem and paying for any costs associated with the error is the responsibility of the

 A. architect
 B. electrical engineer
 C. electrical contractor
 D. general contractor

Solution

AIA Document C401, *Standard Form of Agreement Between Architect and Consultant*, states that consultants are responsible for code compliance regarding their areas of the work. By signing their documents, the consultants become responsible for compliance with applicable codes and regulations.

 Study Note: Review AIA Document C401. Consultants are also responsible for the accurate production of their own drawings and specifications and should check their own documents for consistency. However, from a legal perspective, the architect as prime consultant is liable to the owner for the consultant's work.

The answer is B.

70. An architectural firm is commissioned to remodel a large warehouse building into a multiscreen cinema complex. During the pre-design phase, the architect tells the client that the existing structure must be reviewed and surveyed by the consultants on the design team. Which consultant would be LEAST critical to involve at this time?

 A. civil engineer
 B. structural engineer
 C. mechanical engineer
 D. electrical engineer

Solution

The condition of the major systems and structures of the building would be of most concern during the preliminary examination of the building proposed for remodeling. Any possible civil engineering work, such as site grading, drainage, and the like, could wait until a later time.

The answer is A.

71. An architect suggests that the client contract directly with the structural engineering consultant. A primary reason for suggesting such an arrangement might be because it

 A. gives the architect more control over the consultant's work
 B. permits the consultant to start work earlier
 C. permits the owner to better coordinate the efforts of the project team
 D. relieves the architect of responsibility for paying the consultant

Solution

When an owner contracts directly with a consultant, the architect is not involved with contract provisions, contract disputes, or payment to the consultant. However, the architect sacrifices some control over the consultant's services by not contracting directly with the consultant.

The answer is D.

72. A client discovers shortly after hiring an architect for programming and design services that the client must move out of its existing facility sooner than expected. The new schedule requires that construction and move-in be completed in 18 months instead of the original 21 months. Which recommendation from the architect is the most feasible?

 A. Consider fast-track construction.
 B. Use CPM scheduling and use a negotiated contract rather than bidding the project.
 C. Assign more staff in the architect's office to programming and design and work overtime to get construction started earlier.
 D. Suggest that the client streamline its decision-making process and hire a construction manager.

Solution

Reducing the total time by three months means about a 15% reduction. Fast-track construction would probably take this amount of time off the process.

CPM scheduling would not help much, and negotiation rather than bidding would reduce the time a little, but certainly not by three months. In addition, negotiation would most likely result in a higher cost to the client. Adding more people to the design process would only help a little, and overtime is generally not efficient. Streamlining the decision-making process would not reduce the time required and would probably not be acceptable to the client.

The answer is A.

73. Which of the following statements is true?

   A. An owner has an exclusive license to reproduce drawings for the contractor's use in building the project.

   B. An owner may assign the license to the instruments of service to a lender if it is a condition of financing.

   C. If an architect is found to have defaulted on the Owner-Architect Agreement, the owner receives a nonexclusive license to reproduce the instruments of service and may authorize another architect to complete the project.

   D. An owner may use the instruments of service from a project for an addition or renovation to that project.

Solution

AIA Document B101, Article 7, addresses issues related to the instruments of service. The instruments of service include sketches, drawings, models, specifications, CAD files, and any other deliverables that help move a project from an idea to a real building.

Section 7.3 grants the owner a nonexclusive license to the instruments of service for the purposes of constructing the project, which means that the owner may reproduce the documents as necessary to facilitate construction. If the agreement is terminated, the license is terminated and the architect retains ownership of the documents. If the architect is judged to be in default by a court or arbitration board, the owner is given a new, nonexclusive right to copy the documents and may use them to complete the project with the assistance of another architect.

Section 7.4 states that the owner may not assign his or her license to any other party without the architect's consent.

The answer is C.

74. What is a utilization ratio?

   A. a measure of an employee's billable time versus overhead time

   B. a comparison between programmed and non-programmed spaces

   C. a calculation of the efficiency of a mechanical system

   D. a way to express the buildable area of a site

Solution

A *utilization ratio* is used by firms to determine the amount of time spent on billable work as a percentage of total time for which an employee is compensated. A utilization ratio can be used in an analysis of the profitability and financial standing of a firm. It is calculated by dividing direct hours (or hours billed to projects) by total hours. Generally, employees at lower levels in the firm (drafters, interns, etc.) have higher utilization ratios than project architects and partners, who likely devote a portion of their time to overhead activities such as firm management and marketing.

The answer is A.

75. AIA documents concerning architect/consultant agreements are found in the

   A. C-series
   B. D-series
   C. E-series
   D. G-series

Solution

AIA documents are clustered according to the type of agreements included, as follows.

A-series	owner/general contractor
B-series	owner/architect
C-series	other agreements (including architect/consultant and joint ventures)
D-series	miscellaneous documents
E-series	exhibits
F-series	(reserved for future use)
G-series	contract administration and project management forms (e.g., bid documents log, change order, construction change directive)

The answer is A.

76. According to AIA Document A201, the party responsible for determining the time limits for construction is the

   A. owner
   B. contractor
   C. architect
   D. contractor and subcontractors

Solution

The owner is responsible for determining the time limits for construction; this requirement should be stated in the contract documents. According to AIA Document A201, Sec. 3.10.1, the contractor is responsible for developing a construction schedule that documents the sequence of the work and will allow the project to be completed within the owner's time frame. This schedule is to be submitted to the owner and architect for information only.

The answer is A.

77. During the renovation of an office complex, a fire causes damage to a tenant space. Investigation determines that the fire was caused by a panel box that was not installed according to the manufacturer's instructions. The owner's insurance company compensates the building owner for the cost of the repairs. The insurance company then sues the general contractor and the electrical contractor. The insurance company gains the right to make a claim against the installer in this situation through

  A. limited liability
  B. subrogation
  C. indemnification
  D. negligence

Solution

Subrogation is the legal technique whereby an insurer "steps into the shoes" of a party to whom it has made payment. The building owner has the right to try to collect compensation for the fire damage from the parties at fault. But when the insurance company pays the owner for the cost of repairing the damage, the company is *subrogated* to this right of the owner, and may sue the contractors in the owner's name. The insurer in this situation is called the *subrogee*; the insured party is the *subrogor*.

AIA Document A201, Sec. 11.3.7, encourages the use of a *waiver of subrogation* clause in construction contracts in order to maintain relationships among project participants and minimize the opportunity for lawsuits. By agreeing to such a clause, the parties waive their rights against each other for any damage during construction that is covered by insurance. The rights obtained by the subrogee (the insurance company) cannot be any greater than the rights held originally by the subrogor (the owner), so if an owner and contractor have waived these rights in the contract between them, these rights cannot pass to the insurance company through subrogation.

Parties to such a contract must ensure that the waiver of subrogation clause does not conflict with the requirements of their insurance policies.

The answer is B.

78. Only one of these statements about construction managers is true. Which one?

  A. If an owner brings an independent construction manager into a project shortly before construction begins in order to help "value engineer" the project, the architect's responsibilities and fees are not affected.
  B. A construction manager is often hired when a project has fast-tracked multiple prime construction contracts rather than one general contract for construction.
  C. A construction manager serving as an advisor to an owner during the design development phase is responsible for estimating the construction cost and guaranteeing a maximum price for the work.
  D. AIA Documents A101 and A201 can be used as the agreement between the owner and construction manager.

Solution

A construction manager, or CM, is a benefit to a project with fast-tracked multiple prime contracts, particularly when the owner is not interested in or does not have the experience for coordinating all the parties working on site.

The *Architect's Handbook of Professional Practice* lists a variety of scenarios in which use of a construction manager tends to be most beneficial to the owner.

- projects with fast-tracked multiple prime contracts

- projects that the CM joins early in the design phase, so that the owner can take advantage of the CM's construction expertise while building details are being developed, minimizing the risk that major revisions will be needed to the construction documents later in the process

- projects in which the owner is willing to deal with multiple professionals

- projects in which the CM is sensitive to the relationship between the architect and owner and does not try to come between the two

A construction manager may act either as an advisor to the owner or as a construction contractor. The difference is significant. In the role of advisor, the CM has no direct financial responsibility for the project. In the role of construction contractor, however, the CM is responsible for delivering a finished product for the agreed-on price.

Bringing an independent construction manager into a project often changes the responsibilities of the architect. The CM may take on many of the construction administration tasks traditionally performed by the architect. In addition, the CM's suggestions for cost-cutting may involve revisions to the design and contract documents. When a new player is added to a project team, all people involved should reevaluate their lists of responsibilities and proposed fees and clarify who is now responsible for each item.

The American Institute of Architects (AIA) publishes the CM-Adviser family of documents, which are for use when a CM serves as an adviser to the owner, and the CM-Constructor family, for use when a CM is financially responsible for delivering the project within the guaranteed price.

The answer is B.

PROJECT BUDGET AND FINANCING

79. A building project has just been completed in city A at a cost of $3,000,000. An identical building is planned for city B. A published cost index indicates an index of 1250 for construction in city A and an index of 1350 for construction in city B. The same index suggests that inflation will increase 2% by the time construction of the building in city B is completed. Approximately how much should be budgeted for construction of the building in city B?

    A. $3,180,000
    B. $3,300,000
    C. $3,305,000
    D. $3,366,000

Solution

First determine the multiplying factor.

$$\text{cost index factor} = \frac{\text{cost index of city B}}{\text{cost index of city A}}$$
$$= \frac{1350}{1250}$$
$$= 1.08$$

Multiply this factor by the project cost in city A.

$$\begin{aligned}\text{cost of similar project in city B} &= (\text{cost in city A}) \\ &\quad \times (\text{cost index factor}) \\ &= (\$3,000,000)(1.08) \\ &= \$3,240,000\end{aligned}$$

Finally, increase for inflation.

$$\begin{aligned}\text{budget after inflation} &= (\text{cost in city B}) \\ &\quad \times (\text{inflation factor}) \\ &= (\$3,240,000)(1.02) \\ &= \$3,304,800 \ (\$3,305,000)\end{aligned}$$

There are two other methods that can be used to achieve the same result. Inflation can be calculated first and then the cost index factor can be used, or the inflation factor and cost index factor can be multiplied and applied to the cost in city A.

Study Note: Cost indexes are commonly used on the ARE. Variations on this type of question may include just using indexes without other factors, such as inflation. The examinee may also be asked to find the cost in a city with a lower index. In this case, the factor will be a decimal number less than one.

The answer is C.

80. Which of the following need NOT be accounted for in a project development budget?

    A. professional services
    B. debt service
    C. site development
    D. a contingency

Solution

Debt service is the cost to pay off the construction loan for a project and is generally considered an ongoing cost over many years, not part of the original cost of the project.

The answer is B.

81.   During the programming process for a building project, the client asks the architect to diffuse costs by building in stages. The architect should identify this requirement as which of the following programming concepts?

   A.   flexibility
   B.   phasing
   C.   expansibility
   D.   priority

Solution

The concept of phasing states that a project must be completed in stages to accommodate cost or time constraints.

> *Study Note:* Know all of the 24 programmatic concepts listed in the book *Problem Seeking*, by William M. Peña.

The answer is B.

82.   A published cost index gives a figure of 1440 to construction in city A and 1517 to construction in city B. The same index suggests that inflation will increase by 5% by the midpoint of a project's construction. The project is now budgeted to cost $1,500,000 in city A. Approximately how much should be budgeted for an identical project in city B?

   A. $1,430,000
   B. $1,500,000
   C. $1,660,000
   D. $1,720,000

Solution

There are a number of ways of arriving at the same answer for this question. City B has a higher cost index, so divide the lower into the higher.

$$\frac{1517}{1440} = 1.053$$

Multiply this factor by the cost in city A ($1,500,000) to get $1,579,500. Then increase this by the 5% inflation factor.

($1,579,500)(1.05) = $1,658,475   ($1,660,000)

Alternately, increase for inflation first, then use the cost index factor.

The answer is C.

83.   Contractor's overhead and profit typically amount to what percentage of the construction cost?

   A.   5% to 15%
   B.   10% to 20%
   C.   15% to 30%
   D.   15% to 40%

Solution

Contractor's overhead and profit are typically 15% to 40% of the construction cost.

The answer is D.

84.   A school district is planning a new elementary school to replace an outdated facility. A preliminary budget made during programming has shown that the available funds set aside for the school have been exceeded by 8%. What should the architect do?

I.   Suggest that additional funds from other school building projects be used.

II.   Review the design from a value engineering standpoint for approval by the client to see if costs can be reduced without sacrificing quality.

III. Discuss with the client the possibility of reducing the required area.

IV.   Modify the statement of need concerning the desired level of finish and construction quality on noncritical portions of the facility after consultation with the client.

V.   Propose that building be postponed for a school term until more money can be allocated.

   A.   V, then IV
   B.   III, then IV
   C.   II, then III
   D.   IV, then I

Solution

Because the amount is only 8%, this could probably be made up through a slight reduction in area (statement III) and modifying some levels of quality (statement IV).

Because it is only the programming phase, value engineering is not possible. School districts cannot borrow money from other accounts and usually need to have schools completed as originally scheduled.

The answer is B.

85. The architect typically has the LEAST control over which element of project cost?

    A. escalation budget
    B. percentage of site work relative to building costs
    C. professional fees and consultant services
    D. financing costs

Solution

Financing costs are set by the owner's lender and the architect has no control over this fee.

The architect can, of course, control his or her own fees and, to a certain extent, can negotiate with consultants, so option C is incorrect. Because the architect can control building costs and site work through design, option B is not correct. Although the rate of escalation cannot be controlled, the amount depends on the base cost of construction, which can be controlled through design.

The answer is D.

86. A developer who is purchasing farmland to convert to a housing development would most likely finance the project with a

    A. bridge loan
    B. mezzanine loan
    C. blanket loan
    D. conventional mortgage

Solution

A *blanket loan* is a common tool of developers and is used for the purchase of land that a developer intends to subdivide and resell. Generally it includes a clause that releases each subdivided plot from the loan as it is purchased and a portion of the debt is repaid.

A *bridge loan* is a short-term loan used to close quickly on a property or to finance a project that must begin immediately while waiting for another lender to approve a long-term loan. A *hard money loan* is similar and is based on the value of the property against which the loan is made. The amount of the loan depends on the quick-sale value of the property or the loan-to-value ratio.

Mezzanine loans, which are often used by developers, are large loans with a variable interest rate that increases substantially near the time that the repayment is due. Stock in the developer's company is used as collateral, as opposed to a conventional loan, where the property itself would serve as collateral. The loan requires a gamble that the property will produce enough revenue to repay the loan when the interest rates escalate.

A *conventional mortgage*, which may have either a fixed or adjustable interest rate, is secured by the property purchased. The party borrowing the money agrees to repay the loan over a period of time, and when the debt is repaid, the borrower has clear title to the property. If the borrower defaults, the lender may begin foreclosure and seize the property.

The answer is C.

87. On average, where do construction costs tend to be lowest?

    A. in urban areas
    B. in suburbs
    C. in rural areas
    D. construction costs for a project are the same regardless of the locale

Solution

Construction costs tend to be lowest in suburban areas. Workers in urban areas tend to demand higher wage rates, escalating the cost, while access and transportation to remote rural areas can also force the cost to rise. Suburban areas are generally well connected to urban areas by major transportation routes, but they are not so remote that the cost of transporting materials from the city to the site becomes prohibitive.

The answer is B.

88. Which of the following has the greatest impact on labor costs?

    A. a requirement to use union labor
    B. prime interest rate
    C. the geographic location of the project
    D. overhead

Solution

Labor unions have been a part of the United States economy since the country was founded. These organizations of workers, which began in the colonial era as systems of guilds, strive to improve working conditions, benefits, and wage rates for their membership.

However, the demands of labor unions come with a price, often raising the cost of labor and making union labor much more expensive than labor offered by open shops (businesses that use nonunion workers). This can put a contractor who uses union labor at a disadvantage when competing with a nonunion contractor on a project out for bid. If use of union labor is required by the owner, such as on some public construction projects, prices for the work may be significantly higher.

The other three answer choices have much less or no impact on labor costs. Interest rates affect the volume of construction as a whole, which in turn may affect the prices of labor and materials. Labor rates can vary by geographic location, and the cost of labor in suburban areas tends to be lower than in urban or extremely rural areas. Neither of these affects labor costs as much as a requirement to use union labor does. Overhead costs are not considered to be part of labor costs and are not included in calculations of labor rates.

The answer is A.

SITE ZONING VIGNETTE

Directions

The site plan shows an existing property that has been divided into two new lots. Based on a variety of regulatory and developmental requirements, draw the area suitable for surface improvements and the area suitable for construction of buildings only.

On the grid below the site plan, draw the profile of the existing grade at section A-A shown on the site plan, and draw the profile of the maximum building envelope for each lot based on the program restrictions.

Before beginning, review the program, the code information, and the site plan.

Program

1. On the plan, show the portion of the site where surface improvements are allowed and indicate them with a dashed line. (Note: On the actual exam, there is a *secondary construction area* tool for this purpose.)

2. On the plan, show the portions of the site where building construction is allowed and crosshatch them. (Note: On the actual exam, there is a *buildable area* tool for this purpose.)

3. On the grid, draw the profile of the existing grade at section A-A. (On the actual exam, there is a *grade* tool for this purpose.)

4. On the grid, draw the profile of the maximum building envelope for each lot at section A-A. (On the actual exam, there is a *building profile* tool for this purpose.)

Code Information

The regulatory and developmental constraints are as follows.

- Surface improvements are prohibited within 5 ft (1.5 m) of any property line.

- Surface improvements are not allowed within any easement.

- Construction of surface improvements and buildings is prohibited within 20 ft (6.1 m) of the edge of the highway easement.

- Construction of buildings is prohibited within the building setbacks as follows.

  front setback (Howe Street): 25 ft (7.6 m)

  side setbacks: 15 ft (4.6 m)

  rear setback (north property line): 10 ft (3 m)

- The maximum building height limit within 40 ft (12.2 m) of the west property line is 30 ft (9.1 m) above the allowable west building line.

- The maximum building height of any portion of a building on Lot A is 75 ft (22.9 m) above the average grade level at the building line.

- The maximum building height of structures on Lot B is 60 ft (18.3 m) above the benchmark elevation.

- The maximum building envelope on Lot B is limited to an elevation defined by a 35° line rising from west to east beginning at a point 20 ft (6.1 m) above the building line at grade.

Tips

- Use the sketch tools to lay out each individual restriction.
- Draw the secondary construction area before the buildable area.
- On the actual exam, if one element of two overlapping elements cannot be selected, keep clicking without moving the mouse until the desired element is highlighted.

Tools

Useful tools include the following.

- *zoom* tool for checking setbacks and adjusting elements
- sketch grid to measure required setbacks
- full-screen cursor to help line up grade contours or other elements

Target Time: 1 hour

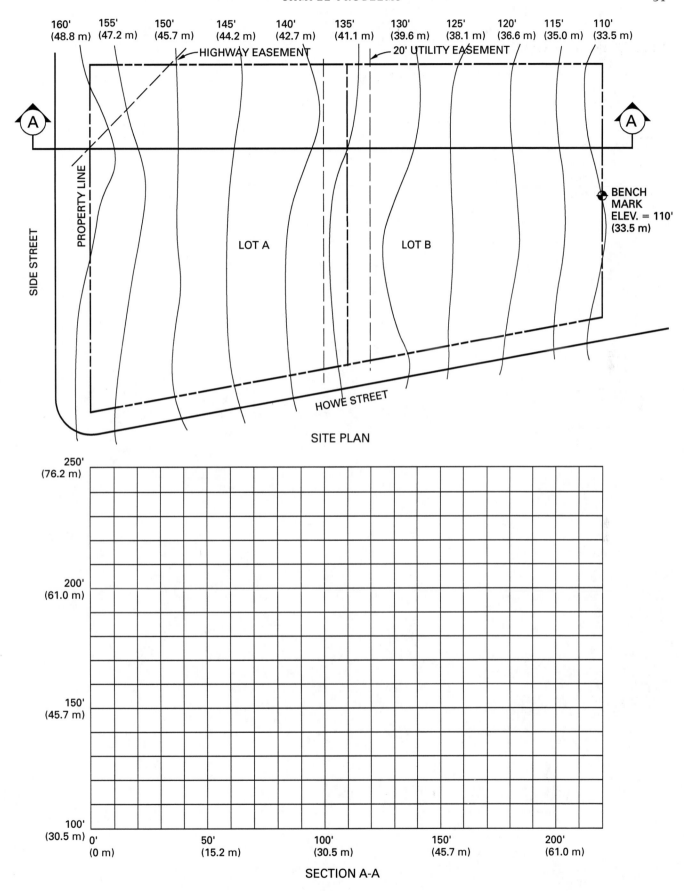

160' (48.8 m)   155' (47.2 m)   150' (45.7 m)   145' (44.2 m)   140' (42.7 m)   135' (41.1 m)   130' (39.6 m)   125' (38.1 m)   120' (36.6 m)   115' (35.0 m)   110' (33.5 m)

HIGHWAY EASEMENT   20' UTILITY EASEMENT

A   A

PROPERTY LINE

SIDE STREET

LOT A   LOT B

BENCH MARK ELEV. = 110' (33.5 m)

HOWE STREET

SITE PLAN

250' (76.2 m)

200' (61.0 m)

150' (45.7 m)

100' (30.5 m)   0' (0 m)   50' (15.2 m)   100' (30.5 m)   150' (45.7 m)   200' (61.0 m)

SECTION A-A

Scale: 1" = 40'-0" (1:500 metric)

SITE ZONING

SITE ZONING: PASSING SOLUTION

In this solution all the setbacks are correctly indicated, and the buildable area is crosshatched, with the correct setback from the highway easement. All other restrictions have been satisfied.

This solution shows the correct grade line profile and correctly maintains the required setbacks and height restrictions. The diagonal building envelope line also begins with the correct starting point.

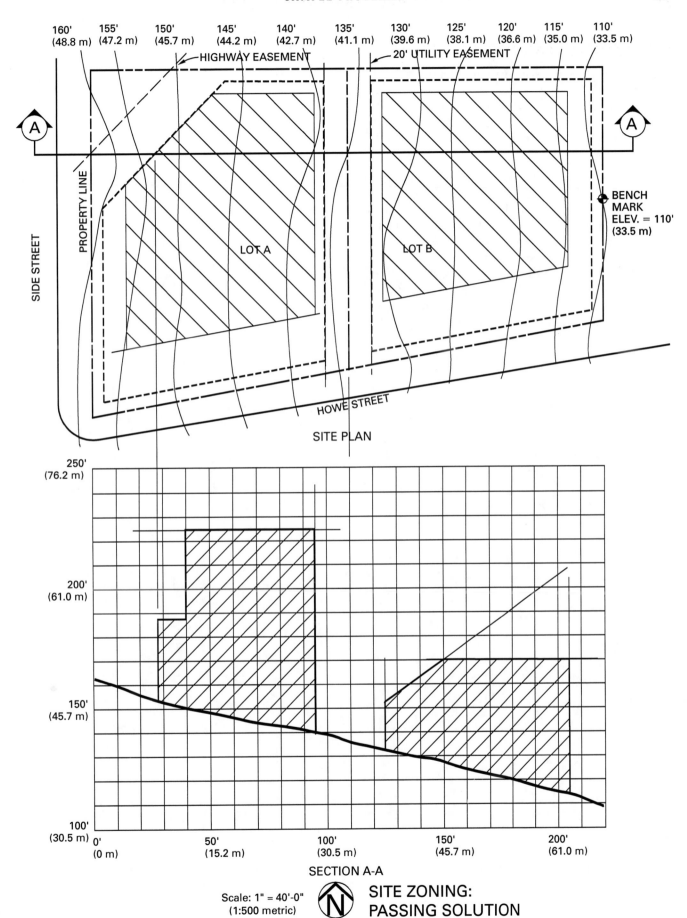

160' (48.8 m) 155' (47.2 m) 150' (45.7 m) 145' (44.2 m) 140' (42.7 m) 135' (41.1 m) 130' (39.6 m) 125' (38.1 m) 120' (36.6 m) 115' (35.0 m) 110' (33.5 m)

HIGHWAY EASEMENT

20' UTILITY EASEMENT

PROPERTY LINE

SIDE STREET

BENCH MARK ELEV. = 110' (33.5 m)

LOT A

LOT B

HOWE STREET

SITE PLAN

250' (76.2 m)

200' (61.0 m)

150' (45.7 m)

100' (30.5 m)

0' (0 m)   50' (15.2 m)   100' (30.5 m)   150' (45.7 m)   200' (61.0 m)

SECTION A-A

Scale: 1" = 40'-0" (1:500 metric)

SITE ZONING: PASSING SOLUTION

SITE ZONING: FAILING SOLUTION

There are two major problems with the solution on the site plan. The surface improvements line is incorrectly drawn 5 ft (1.5 m) from the highway easement instead of 20 ft (6.1 m) as required by the program. The building line along Howe Street has also been mistakenly drawn 25 ft (7.6 m) from the curb line instead of from the property line.

This solution has three major errors in the section. First, the diagonal building envelope line on Lot B has been taken from the property line instead of the building line, resulting in a larger building envelope than is allowed. Second, the 75 ft (22.9 m) maximum building height on Lot A has been incorrectly established from the east building line rather than from the average grade level, which adds 10 ft (3 m) to the allowable height. Third, the west edge of the building line on Lot A has been drawn at the setback from the west property line instead of at the point where the section line A-A crosses the setback from the highway easement.

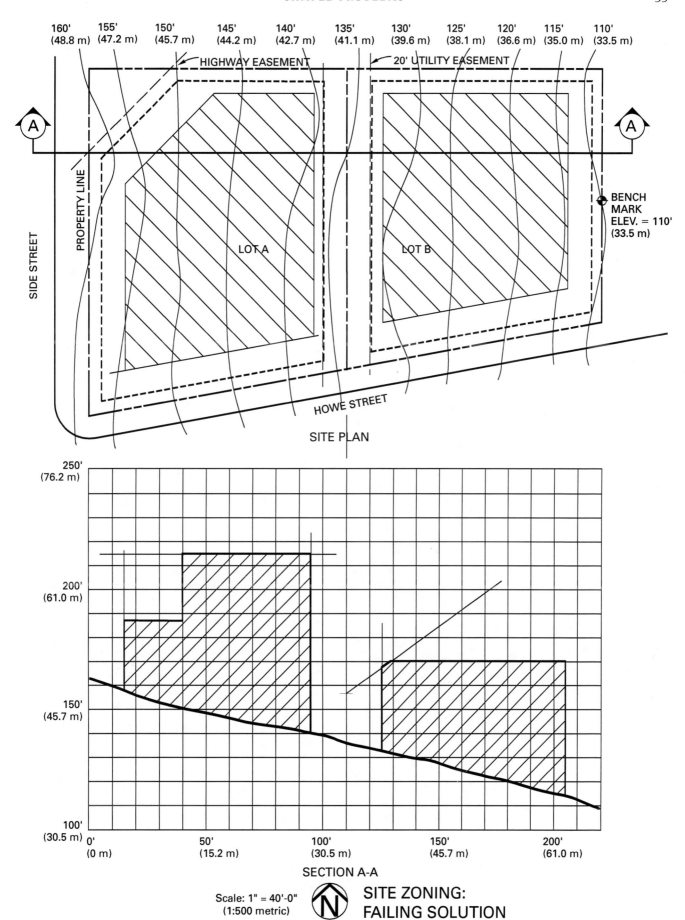

160'
(48.8 m)
155'
(47.2 m)
150'
(45.7 m)
145'
(44.2 m)
140'
(42.7 m)
135'
(41.1 m)
130'
(39.6 m)
125'
(38.1 m)
120'
(36.6 m)
115'
(35.0 m)
110'
(33.5 m)

HIGHWAY EASEMENT

20' UTILITY EASEMENT

A

A

BENCH
MARK
ELEV. = 110'
(33.5 m)

PROPERTY LINE

SIDE STREET

LOT A

LOT B

HOWE STREET

SITE PLAN

250'
(76.2 m)

200'
(61.0 m)

150'
(45.7 m)

100'
(30.5 m)

0'
(0 m)

50'
(15.2 m)

100'
(30.5 m)

150'
(45.7 m)

200'
(61.0 m)

SECTION A-A

Scale: 1" = 40'-0"
(1:500 metric)

N

SITE ZONING:
FAILING SOLUTION

PRACTICE EXAM: MULTIPLE CHOICE

Directions

Reference books should not be used on this practice exam. Besides this book, you should have only a calculator, pencils, and scratch paper. (On the actual exam, these will be provided and should not be brought into the site.)

Target Time: 2 hours

1.	Ⓐ Ⓑ Ⓒ Ⓓ	26.	Ⓐ Ⓑ Ⓒ Ⓓ	51.	Ⓐ Ⓑ Ⓒ Ⓓ
2.	Ⓐ Ⓑ Ⓒ Ⓓ	27.	Ⓐ Ⓑ Ⓒ Ⓓ	52.	Ⓐ Ⓑ Ⓒ Ⓓ
3.	Ⓐ Ⓑ Ⓒ Ⓓ	28.	Ⓐ Ⓑ Ⓒ Ⓓ	53.	Ⓐ Ⓑ Ⓒ Ⓓ
4.	Ⓐ Ⓑ Ⓒ Ⓓ	29.	Ⓐ Ⓑ Ⓒ Ⓓ	54.	Ⓐ Ⓑ Ⓒ Ⓓ
5.	Ⓐ Ⓑ Ⓒ Ⓓ	30.	Ⓐ Ⓑ Ⓒ Ⓓ	55.	Ⓐ Ⓑ Ⓒ Ⓓ
6.	Ⓐ Ⓑ Ⓒ Ⓓ	31.	_____	56.	Ⓐ Ⓑ Ⓒ Ⓓ
7.	Ⓐ Ⓑ Ⓒ Ⓓ	32.	Ⓐ Ⓑ Ⓒ Ⓓ	57.	Ⓐ Ⓑ Ⓒ Ⓓ
8.	Ⓐ Ⓑ Ⓒ Ⓓ	33.	Ⓐ Ⓑ Ⓒ Ⓓ	58.	Ⓐ Ⓑ Ⓒ Ⓓ
9.	Ⓐ Ⓑ Ⓒ Ⓓ	34.	Ⓐ Ⓑ Ⓒ Ⓓ	59.	Ⓐ Ⓑ Ⓒ Ⓓ
10.	Ⓐ Ⓑ Ⓒ Ⓓ	35.	Ⓐ Ⓑ Ⓒ Ⓓ	60.	Ⓐ Ⓑ Ⓒ Ⓓ
11.	Ⓐ Ⓑ Ⓒ Ⓓ	36.	Ⓐ Ⓑ Ⓒ Ⓓ	61.	Ⓐ Ⓑ Ⓒ Ⓓ
12.	Ⓐ Ⓑ Ⓒ Ⓓ	37.	Ⓐ Ⓑ Ⓒ Ⓓ	62.	Ⓐ Ⓑ Ⓒ Ⓓ
13.	Ⓐ Ⓑ Ⓒ Ⓓ	38.	Ⓐ Ⓑ Ⓒ Ⓓ	63.	Ⓐ Ⓑ Ⓒ Ⓓ
14.	Ⓐ Ⓑ Ⓒ Ⓓ	39.	Ⓐ Ⓑ Ⓒ Ⓓ	64.	Ⓐ Ⓑ Ⓒ Ⓓ
15.	Ⓐ Ⓑ Ⓒ Ⓓ Ⓔ Ⓕ	40.	Ⓐ Ⓑ Ⓒ Ⓓ	65.	Ⓐ Ⓑ Ⓒ Ⓓ Ⓔ Ⓕ
16.	Ⓐ Ⓑ Ⓒ Ⓓ	41.	Ⓐ Ⓑ Ⓒ Ⓓ	66.	Ⓐ Ⓑ Ⓒ Ⓓ
17.	Ⓐ Ⓑ Ⓒ Ⓓ	42.	Ⓐ Ⓑ Ⓒ Ⓓ	67.	Ⓐ Ⓑ Ⓒ Ⓓ
18.	Ⓐ Ⓑ Ⓒ Ⓓ	43.	Ⓐ Ⓑ Ⓒ Ⓓ	68.	Ⓐ Ⓑ Ⓒ Ⓓ
19.	Ⓐ Ⓑ Ⓒ Ⓓ	44.	Ⓐ Ⓑ Ⓒ Ⓓ	69.	Ⓐ Ⓑ Ⓒ Ⓓ
20.	Ⓐ Ⓑ Ⓒ Ⓓ	45.	Ⓐ Ⓑ Ⓒ Ⓓ	70.	Ⓐ Ⓑ Ⓒ Ⓓ
21.	Ⓐ Ⓑ Ⓒ Ⓓ	46.	Ⓐ Ⓑ Ⓒ Ⓓ	71.	Ⓐ Ⓑ Ⓒ Ⓓ
22.	Ⓐ Ⓑ Ⓒ Ⓓ Ⓔ Ⓕ	47.	Ⓐ Ⓑ Ⓒ Ⓓ	72.	Ⓐ Ⓑ Ⓒ Ⓓ
23.	Ⓐ Ⓑ Ⓒ Ⓓ	48.	Ⓐ Ⓑ Ⓒ Ⓓ	73.	Ⓐ Ⓑ Ⓒ Ⓓ
24.	Ⓐ Ⓑ Ⓒ Ⓓ	49.	Ⓐ Ⓑ Ⓒ Ⓓ	74.	Ⓐ Ⓑ Ⓒ Ⓓ
25.	Ⓐ Ⓑ Ⓒ Ⓓ	50.	Ⓐ Ⓑ Ⓒ Ⓓ	75.	Ⓐ Ⓑ Ⓒ Ⓓ

76. Ⓐ Ⓑ Ⓒ Ⓓ
77. ⒶⒷⒸⒹⒺⒻ
78. Ⓐ Ⓑ Ⓒ Ⓓ
79. Ⓐ Ⓑ Ⓒ Ⓓ
80. Ⓐ Ⓑ Ⓒ Ⓓ
81. Ⓐ Ⓑ Ⓒ Ⓓ
82. Ⓐ Ⓑ Ⓒ Ⓓ
83. Ⓐ Ⓑ Ⓒ Ⓓ
84. Ⓐ Ⓑ Ⓒ Ⓓ
85. Ⓐ Ⓑ Ⓒ Ⓓ

1.   In the following illustration, what would be an appropriate use for the sloped region between points A and B?

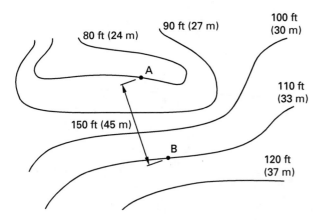

A.   Use it as a parking area.
B.   Plant it with grass.
C.   Use it as a detention area.
D.   Use it as a building site.

2.   Which of the following building types would probably have the lowest efficiency?

A.   a shoe store in a shopping mall
B.   a community library
C.   a hospital
D.   a college chemistry building

3.   A family wishes to add a bedroom and bath to the first floor of their home to accommodate an elderly relative who will move in after she is discharged from a rehabilitation hospital. The family hopes to build the rooms adjacent to an existing but seldom-used sitting room, so that she may have her own living area. The site is tight, and the proposed addition may need to extend 2 ft (610) into the property setback. The homeowners may choose to apply for

A.   an easement
B.   a covenant
C.   a conditional use permit
D.   a variance

4.   The floor area ratio for a suburban property is 2.0. The lot is 50 ft (15 m) wide (parallel to the street) by 100 ft (30 m) deep (perpendicular to the street). The required front setback is 10 ft (3 m), and the back and side setbacks are 5 ft (1.5 m). Which of the following building configurations may be constructed?

A.   a two-story building that is 50 ft (15 m) wide by 100 ft (30 m) deep
B.   a three-story building that is 40 ft (12 m) wide by 80 ft (24 m) deep
C.   a three-story building that is 40 ft (12 m) wide by 85 ft (25.5 m) deep
D.   a four-story building that is 40 ft (12 m) wide by 65 ft (20 m) deep

5.   Of which type of town plan is the following illustration representative?

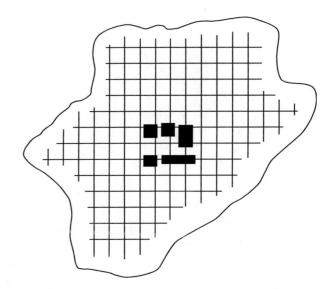

A.   Greek
B.   Roman
C.   medieval
D.   Renaissance

6.   Which of the following architectural works does NOT include anthropomorphic elements?

A.   Nationale-Nederlanden Building
B.   Erechtheum
C.   Casa Mila
D.   Unité d'Habitation

7.   Which is the most accurate method of determining the value of a property?

    A. the development method
    B. the comparison method
    C. the income approach method
    D. the allocation method

8.   An architect is designing a small community theater that will feature musical and spoken word performances. The theater company's artistic director requests that the architect develop a design that will make it possible for the performer to have eye contact with every spectator in the theater while maximizing the number of seats from which the audience can see and hear most clearly. Which diagram represents the best approach to the theater layout?

A.

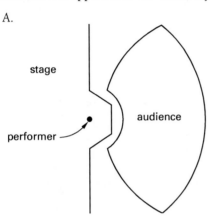

B.

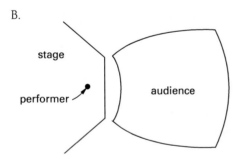

C.

D.

9.   The document that legally describes the layout of a subdivided piece of property is called a

    A. survey
    B. master plan
    C. plat
    D. deed

10.   An old stone mansion, constructed in the 1850s, is purchased by a law firm. The building is eligible for the National Register of Historic Places, and the firm intends to apply for federal tax credits. An architect joins the project to figure out how to fit the attorneys' offices, support spaces, library, and conference rooms into the existing space. In addition, the architect has been asked to survey the existing building and identify any portions of the structure in need of repair. Which of the following recommendations would NOT be appropriate for this facility?

    A.   Remove an existing service stairway, which appears to have been added to the building in the 1970s, and replace it with a new stairway designed to comply with current code require-ments.

    B.   Remove the contemporary carpet in the dining room, strip the white paint from the mahogany paneling, and refinish the wood with a dark stain to approximate the way the room looked in a Civil War era photograph.

    C.   Replace a crumbling plaster medallion on the ceiling of the entry foyer with a new medallion, made from a mold of the existing ornament.

    D.   Remove all of the trim from the interior walls, install furring strips and insulation, replace the plaster, and reinstall the trim.

11.   Which of the following methods of sedimentation control may help to prevent erosion?

    A.   a sediment trap
    B.   permanent seeding and landscaping
    C.   earth dykes
    D.   a silt fence

12.   Which of the following was the first dome to be con-structed without the use of centering?

    A.   Pantheon
    B.   St. Peter's Basilica
    C.   Florence Cathedral
    D.   U.S. Capitol

13.   Absolute title to a portion of a structure is known as

    A.   fee simple ownership
    B.   condominium ownership
    C.   leasehold ownership
    D.   cooperative ownership

14.   Which of the following is NOT a characteristic of partnering?

    A.   Partnering is often used in conjunction with mediation and arbitration to prevent lawsuits.

    B.   Partnering can include project participants other than the owner, contractor, and architect.

    C.   A partnering agreement applies only to the proj-ect at hand.

    D.   A partnering agreement becomes a part of the contract between the architect and owner and the owner and contractor.

15.   According to the following affinity matrix, to which room or rooms must the kitchen be adjacent? (Choose the three that apply.)

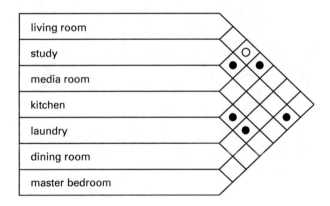

    A.   living room
    B.   study
    C.   media room
    D.   laundry
    E.   dining room
    F.   master bedroom

16. Had Frank Lloyd Wright's Broadacre City concept been widely implemented, a result may have been

    A. increased rehabilitation of old urban neighborhoods, as cities would "patch holes" in the existing fabric before expanding outward

    B. increased suburban sprawl, as more land would be allocated for each residential site and the inhabitants would depend solely on the automobile for transportation

    C. large developments featuring clustered housing in high-rise buildings, surrounded by large amounts of open space

    D. more mixes of residential, commercial, and light industrial uses within one neighborhood and increased use of public transportation systems

17. A property where hazardous substances, pollutants, or contaminants may be present is known as

    A. a condemned property

    B. an urban renewal

    C. a brownfield

    D. an industrial site

18. A method of construction delivery that obtains an early fixed price for a project based on a set of design documents and then gives the contractor responsibility for determining the details of construction is called

    A. design-build

    B. bridging

    C. fast-track

    D. integration

19. Which of the following cost opinions should include the highest contingency allowance?

    A. a cost opinion prepared just before the drawings are sent to contractors for bids on a small veterinary clinic

    B. a cost opinion prepared at the conclusion of the design development phase for an addition to a building designed by the architect two years ago

    C. a cost opinion prepared at the conclusion of the schematic design phase for converting an old warehouse into artists' studios and loft apartments

    D. a cost opinion prepared during the programming phase for a new elementary school

20. Which of the following would NOT be included in an environmental impact statement?

    A. an analysis of a site's historic features

    B. an analysis of a proposed project's energy requirements

    C. a description of all reasonable alternatives to proposed actions

    D. a letter of approval from the Environmental Protection Agency

21. Which organizational pattern for a space best facilitates social interaction?

    A.

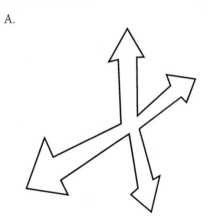

    B.

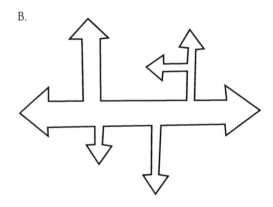

C.

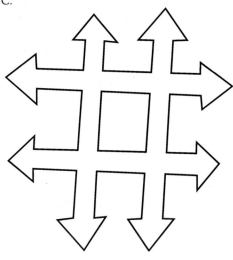

D.

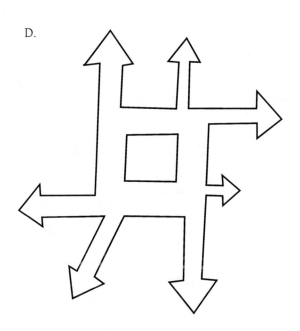

22. Which of the following are likely results of shortening the critical path of a construction schedule? (Choose the two that apply.)

    A. Direct costs will increase.
    B. Direct costs will decrease.
    C. Overhead costs will increase.
    D. Overhead costs will decrease.
    E. Quality control will increase.
    F. Activities on float paths will be delayed.

23. A grocer purchases a corner market in the middle of a historic residential neighborhood. The property includes a small garden and a seating area located beside the store. A clause in the deed requires the grocer to maintain the garden and keep it open to the public. This is an example of

    A. a prescriptive covenant
    B. an affirmative covenant
    C. a conditional covenant
    D. a conditional use permit

24. Which of the following would NOT be included in a contractor's project overhead costs?

    A. transportation expenses
    B. temporary office and sanitary facilities
    C. payroll taxes
    D. permits

25. Which of the following statements regarding eminent domain is FALSE?

    A. Before initiating eminent domain proceedings, the condemnor must offer to buy the property from the owner.
    B. Fair market value of a property is always based on the market data analysis method of valuation.
    C. The power of eminent domain may be delegated to a private, for-profit company.
    D. The right to eminent domain is granted to the government by the Fifth Amendment to the U.S. Constitution.

26. Which of the following statements about property rights is FALSE?

A. Riparian rights give a property owner whose property abuts a river the right to construct means to access the water, such as a boat dock.
B. Air rights give the owner of a property the right to prohibit aircraft from entering that space, such as the protective area around Washington, DC.
C. Littoral rights give the owner of a property along the Gulf of Mexico the right to fish from the shore.
D. A West Virginia mountaineer who discovers oil on his property may sell the subsurface rights to a petroleum company while continuing to live on the property.

27. Which of the following cities was NOT designed according to Baroque town planning principles?

A. London
B. Paris
C. New York City
D. Washington, DC

28. Which of the following does NOT contribute to the size of a building's footprint?

A. use group
B. total gross area
C. number of floors
D. configuration

29. A chef is considering the purchase of an abandoned church, with the intention of turning it into a restaurant. The property's zoning designation allows this type of use. The chef has obtained a preliminary site plan and permission to access the site from the current owner, and hires an architect to assist with a feasibility study to examine the possibility of converting the old building to the new use. Which of the following should the architect do first?

A. Check local zoning ordinances and analyze the site to determine if there is enough space available for the parking required.
B. Assist the restaurateur in developing a program and check the space requirements against the area and layout of the existing structure.
C. Research the history of the church.
D. Complete a code review of the existing building and develop a preliminary plan for renovation.

30. A developer plans to construct an office building on a previously undisturbed site. Each of the buildings shown has the same gross square footage. Which of the following diagrams represents the best planning approach?

A.

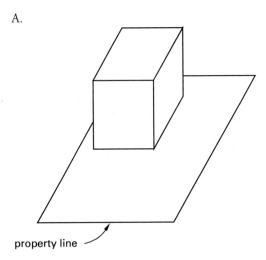

property line

B.

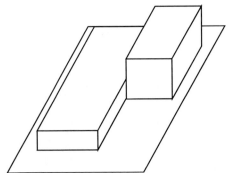

C.

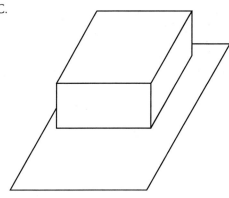

D.

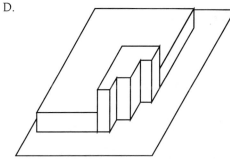

31.   The critical path time for the following CPM diagram is _____ days. (Fill in the blank.)

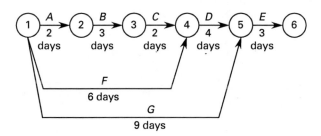

32.   Which of the following statements regarding building costs is FALSE?

    A.   The higher the perimeter-to-floor area ratio, the greater the unit cost.

    B.   The greater the floor-to-floor height, the greater the unit cost.

    C.   The greater the floor area of the building, the greater the unit cost.

    D.   The taller the building, the greater the unit cost.

33.   The height of a classical column is a function of the

    A.   height of a typical man

    B.   diameter of the column

    C.   height of the steps of the temple

    D.   spacing between columns

34.   An architect's cost opinion for a project would NOT include

    A.   professional fees

    B.   hard costs

    C.   contractor's overhead and profit

    D.   contingency allowances

35.   Retainage at substantial completion is frequently equivalent to

    A.   a percentage of incomplete items

    B.   the contractor's overhead

    C.   the cost of bonds

    D.   the contractor's profit

36.   Which of the following factors would increase efficiency?

    A.   a central mechanical plant

    B.   small rooms

    C.   a single-story building

    D.   many offices requiring windows

37.   In the terminology of Kevin Lynch's 1960 book, *The Image of the City*, an area that is perceived as a symbol of a part of a city is a

    A.   node

    B.   landmark

    C.   district

    D.   core

38.   According to *Design with Nature*, Ian McHarg's 1969 book on conservation and site planning, which of the following sites would be most suitable for development?

    A.   forest/woodland

    B.   prime agricultural land

    C.   marshland

    D.   aquifer recharge area

39. An architect is designing a four-story hotel. She wishes to expose the structural system while maintaining a high fire-resistance rating, and she needs to minimize construction time. Which type of framing system should the architect choose?

    A. a wood platform frame
    B. light-gauge steel framing
    C. a steel frame with rigid connections
    D. a one-way solid slab concrete frame

40. For which of the following building types would the room data sheet approach to programming be most appropriate?

    A. a college dormitory
    B. a speculative office building
    C. a high school
    D. an assembly line area of a factory

41. A 100-year flood is defined as

    A. the most significant flood in a 100-year period
    B. a flood level with a 1% probability of being equaled or surpassed each year
    C. the highest water level recorded on a specific site during the past 100 years
    D. an area where development is not permitted

42. An agreement between an architect and his or her consultants must

I. reference the owner-architect agreement
II. require the consultant to carry liability insurance
III. include a provision stating that if the architect is not paid by the owner, the consultant will not be paid
IV. be based on AIA Document C401

    A. I and II only
    B. I and IV only
    C. II, III, and IV only
    D. none of the above

43. An architecture firm is assigning staff to work on a small addition to a library. The principal architect has chosen a project manager and has decided to assign two interns to the job to assist with production. The project manager is developing a schedule for the project based on the available work hours and the client's deadlines. Which type of schedule would be appropriate for this project?

    A. a milestone chart
    B. a bar chart
    C. a Gantt chart
    D. a CPM

44. Le Corbusier's proportioning system, the Modulor, is based on

I. the human body
II. classical orders
III. the golden section
IV. the Japanese ken

    A. III only
    B. I and II only
    C. I and III only
    D. III and IV only

45. Which of the following sustainable design approaches would be LEAST likely to meet a building's safety and security objectives?

    A. parking areas under the building
    B. constructed wetlands
    C. integrated building automation and control systems
    D. Trombe walls

46. Which of the following is NOT a characteristic of the construction management at risk project delivery method?

    A. complete package of construction documents prior to the start of construction
    B. three prime players
    C. two separate contracts
    D. provider selection based on factors other than cost

47. An architect is preparing a cost evaluation for a project during the programming stage. The opinion is based upon a previous, similar project. Which of the following is a known factor that will add cost to the project?

    A. a contingency
    B. a premium
    C. an additive alternate
    D. an upcharge

48. Which of the following configurations of trees would be the most effective windbreak?

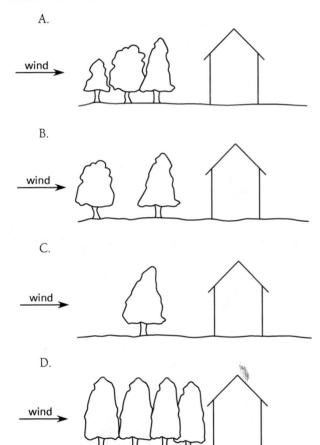

49. Which of the following would indicate an existing contour line on a site plan?

    A.
        250

    B.
        250

    C.
        250

    D.
        250

50. Which of these documents establishes unit prices?

    A. Owner-Contractor Agreement (AIA Document A101)
    B. *General Conditions* (AIA Document A201)
    C. supplementary conditions
    D. special conditions

51. A local hospital is planning a new cardiac care wing. An architect and the hospital's project manager have been working for a year and a half to define the design requirements, and the project is approaching the end of the design development phase. One day, the project manager learned that the hospital had received a gift of $10 million to build the cardiac center, and the hospital board of directors authorized the project manager to do whatever it takes to open the new cardiac center in one year. Which project delivery method would be a good choice in this situation?

    A. design-build
    B. design-bid-build
    C. fast-track
    D. negotiated contract with a guaranteed maximum price

52. What is the intent of defensible space?

    A. to design spaces so that law enforcement can better survey and control a neighborhood
    B. to protect private property owners from vandalism and crime
    C. to allow residents to control the areas around their homes
    D. to mix income levels within housing facilities

53.   Which of the following detains water and allows it to be absorbed slowly by the ground?

    A.   a bioswale

    B.   an infiltration basin

    C.   a catch basin

    D.   a cistern

54.   A town plans to build a small airport for commuter flights to the nearest metropolis. Which public works financing method would be most appropriate to use to fund the project?

    A.   an ad valorem tax

    B.   a general obligation bond

    C.   a development impact fee

    D.   a public enterprise revenue bond

55.   A school district is an example of

    A.   an overlay zoning district

    B.   a catchment area

    C.   a planned unit development

    D.   a neighborhood

56.   For which climate would these four design strategies be appropriate?

- shade openings with moveable awnings
- select dark colors for exterior building finishes
- locate no windows on the north elevation
- use compact forms

    A.   cool

    B.   temperate

    C.   hot-humid

    D.   hot-arid

57.   The net assignable area of a public library is 32,000 ft^2 (3000 m^2). The efficiency of the building is estimated to be about 75%. What should the approximate target gross square footage of the building be?

    A.   24,000 ft^2 (2200 m^2)

    B.   40,000 ft^2 (3700 m^2)

    C.   43,000 ft^2 (4000 m^2)

    D.   44,000 ft^2 (4100 m^2)

58.   A building in Gettysburg, Pennsylvania, figured prominently in the Civil War and is now used as a small private museum. The brick structure is adjacent to a battlefield and has been maintained largely as it was in 1863, with the exception of a small wood frame addition built in the 1960s. The addition is deteriorating and will be removed. This project is an example of which historic building treatment approach?

    A.   rehabilitation

    B.   restoration

    C.   reconstruction

    D.   preservation

59.   During "circle time" in a kindergarten class, the children arrange their chairs in a half circle with the teacher in the center, say their ABCs and count to 10, and read a book. The students then sing a song before going to their tables for snack time. This is an illustration of

    A.   proximetrics

    B.   territoriality

    C.   personalization

    D.   a behavior setting

60.   Which of the following is NOT one of the Secretary of the Interior's Standards for Rehabilitation?

    A.   New additions shall attempt to match the existing structure as closely as possible.

    B.   Properties shall be used for their original purpose or for a new use requiring minimal changes.

    C.   Historic materials shall be repaired rather than replaced whenever possible.

    D.   Historically significant changes shall be preserved.

61.   Which of the following strategies would NOT be employed in a community adopting the principles of defensible space?

    A.   gated streets

    B.   strict enforcement of code regulations

    C.   loan programs for first-time homebuyers

    D.   specification of vandal-resistant materials

62. Which of the following characteristics is NOT required for a space to serve as an area of refuge?

    A. rated fire separation from adjacent spaces
    B. open to the exterior
    C. means of egress from the space
    D. two-way communications

63. A road that connects an interstate to a street on the outskirts of a residential area is known as

    A. an expressway
    B. a local access road
    C. a collector-distributor
    D. an arterial

64. Construction of a hospital in the design phase this summer is expected to begin next fall and be completed two years after notice to proceed is given. As the development budget is prepared, the costs should be escalated to reflect the projected price in

    A. during design
    B. at the start of construction
    C. in the middle of the project
    D. when construction is scheduled to be completed

65. Which of the following determines the allowable height of a building? (Choose the four that apply.)

    A. use group
    B. type of construction
    C. fire-suppression system
    D. means of egress
    E. occupant load
    F. zoning ordinances

66. Which of the following may serve as a required exit?

    A. a fire escape with metal grate treads
    B. an escalator
    C. an elevator
    D. an exterior stairway with solid treads

67. A special design approach and construction method may be required in areas where the water table is less than

    A. 6.0 ft (1.8 m) under the surface
    B. 8.0 ft (2.4 m) under the surface
    C. 10 ft (3.0 m) under the surface
    D. 15 ft (4.6 m) under the surface

68. An architect is planning a site for a complex of office buildings and wishes to specify ground surface materials that will help to moderate the microclimate. To meet this goal, he should specify materials with

    A. high albedo and high conductivity
    B. low albedo and low conductivity
    C. high albedo and low conductivity
    D. low albedo and high conductivity

69. According to AIA Document B101, *Standard Form of Agreement Between Owner and Architect*, who is responsible for developing the program?

    A. the owner
    B. the owner's attorney
    C. the architect
    D. the construction manager

70. Which of the following determines minimum parking requirements for a specific site?

    A. local zoning ordinances
    B. building codes
    C. owner's preferences
    D. *ADA/ABA Guidelines*

71. Which of the following statements regarding joint ventures is FALSE?

    A. A joint venture is limited to a specific project.
    B. A joint venture pays no income taxes and earns no profits.
    C. AIA Document C801 can be used to form a joint venture.
    D. Liability insurance held by one of the parties will cover both parties involved in a joint venture.

72.   In the programming phase of a project, which of the following would have the LEAST impact on a cost projection?

    A.   the client's needs
    B.   the client's timing
    C.   market conditions
    D.   site requirements

73.   A shopping center featuring a large grocery store, a few small take-out restaurants, a variety store, a greeting card shop, and a video rental store would be classified as a

    A.   neighborhood center
    B.   community center
    C.   regional center
    D.   market center

74.   A small business owner plans to build a factory and small warehouse to manufacture and distribute her line of diaper bags. She negotiates a $75,000 loan to supplement the funds contributed by investors. Which calculation would be used to determine how much her monthly payments will be if she intends to repay the loan in 10 years?

    A.   uniform present worth
    B.   uniform sinking fund
    C.   life-cycle cost analysis
    D.   uniform capital recovery

75.   Which of the following is NOT a tenet of Crime Prevention Through Environmental Design?

    A.   Provide clear transitions between public and private spaces.
    B.   Provide windows for tenant surveillance.
    C.   Place safe activity in safe locations.
    D.   Locate stairways near heavily used areas.

76.   Which of the following soil types has the steepest angle of repose?

    A.   sand
    B.   clay
    C.   silt
    D.   a mixture of sand, silt, and clay

77.   Which of the following would generally be required to comply with a site setback? (Choose the four that apply.)

    A.   a bay window
    B.   a roof overhang
    C.   a fence
    D.   a detached garage
    E.   landscaping
    F.   a deck

78.   Which foundation strategy LEAST disturbs natural surface drainage patterns?

    A.   piles
    B.   a raised pad
    C.   a stepped foundation
    D.   earthen berms

79.   The science of designing objects and spaces so that they can be used most efficiently and comfortably by people is called

    A.   anthropomorphism
    B.   ergonomics
    C.   primogentrics
    D.   bionomics

80.   Whose writings represent retaliation against the modern architecture of the 1950s and 1960s and advocate owner-directed selection of program concepts?

    A.   Kenneth Frampton
    B.   Christopher Alexander
    C.   William Peña
    D.   Kevin Lynch

81.   Which of the following was excluded from Tony Garnier's proposal for a *cité industrielle*?

    A.   reinforced concrete structures
    B.   religious buildings
    C.   tree-lined pedestrian paths through the city
    D.   zoning regulations

...tatements is true regarding

...e more likely to be affected ...an fine-grained soils.

...nd clay would have a ...y for a small residence.

...ter to migrate above the

...ould be placed above the ...t be affected by heaving.

...lding shapes would be ...ot-humid climate?

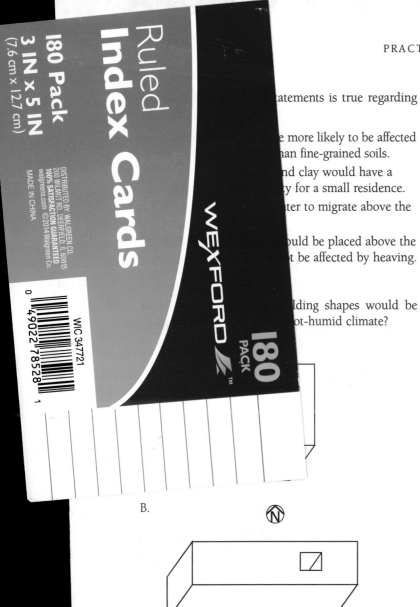

B.

C.

D.

84. Drafting and redrafting a program until two parties agree, with a programmer acting as intermediary, is known as

   A. groupthink

   B. brainstorming

   C. lateral thinking

   D. shuttle diplomacy

85. The approach to town planning known as "new urbanism" advocates three of the following design strategies. Which one is NOT a hallmark of new urbanism?

   A. narrow streets and frequent intersections

   B. mixed-use occupancies, such as apartments over retail shops

   C. parallel parking

   D. office parks

PRACTICE EXAM: VIGNETTE

⋈⋈⋈

SITE ZONING

Directions

The site plan shows an existing property that has been divided into two new lots. Based on a variety of regulatory and developmental requirements, draw the area suitable for surface improvements and the area suitable for construction of buildings only.

On the grid below the site plan, draw the profile of the existing grade at the section cut shown on the site plan, and draw the profile of the maximum building envelope for each lot based on the program restrictions.

Before beginning, review the program, the code information, and the site plan.

Program

1. On the plan, show the portions of the site where surface improvements are allowed and indicate them with a solid line. (On the actual exam, there is a *secondary construction area* tool for this purpose.)

2. On the plan, show the portions of the site where building construction is allowed and indicate them with a dashed line. (On the actual exam, there is a *buildable area* tool for this purpose.)

3. On the grid, draw the profile of the existing grade at section A-A. (On the actual exam, there is a *grade* tool for this purpose.)

4. On the grid, draw the profile of the maximum building envelope for each lot at section A-A using a heavy line. (On the actual exam, there is a *building profile* tool for this purpose.)

Code Information

The regulatory and developmental constraints are as follows.

- Surface improvements are prohibited within 5 ft (1.5 m) of any property line.
- Construction of buildings is prohibited within the building setbacks, which are measured from the property lines of the two lots.

  front setback along Front Street: 20 ft (6 m)

  rear setback: 15 ft (4.5 m)

  side setbacks: 10 ft (3 m)

- Construction of buildings and other surface improvements is prohibited within 30 ft (9 m) of the park boundary.
- Construction of buildings is prohibited within the existing open space easement.
- The maximum building height limit is 70 ft (21 m) above the benchmark elevation.
- The maximum building height limit within 50 ft (15 m) of the west property line of Lot A shall be 20 ft (6 m) above grade at the property line.
- The maximum building height limit within 60 ft (18 m) of the east property line of Lot B shall be 60 ft (18 m) above the benchmark elevation.
- The maximum building envelope is restricted to an elevation defined by a 30° line rising westward from a point 30 ft (9 m) directly above the benchmark.

Tips

- Use the sketch tools to lay out each individual restriction.
- Draw the secondary construction area before the buildable area.

- On the actual exam, if one element of two overlapping elements cannot be selected, keep clicking without moving the mouse until the desired element is highlighted.

Tools

Useful tools include the following.

- *zoom* tool for checking setbacks and adjusting elements
- sketch grid to measure required setbacks
- full-screen cursor to help line up grade contours or other elements

Target Time: 1 hour

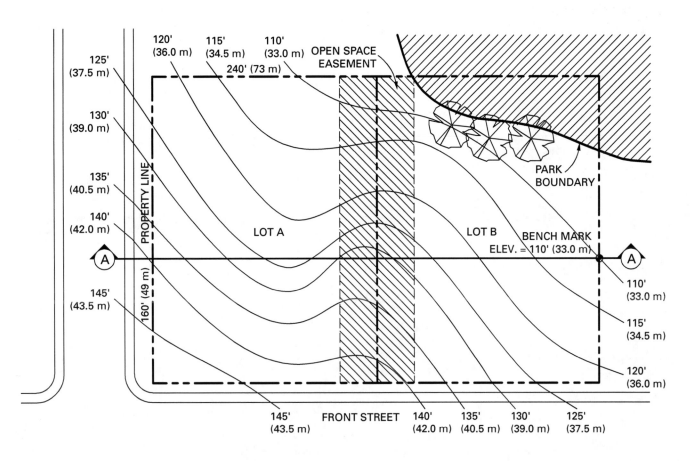

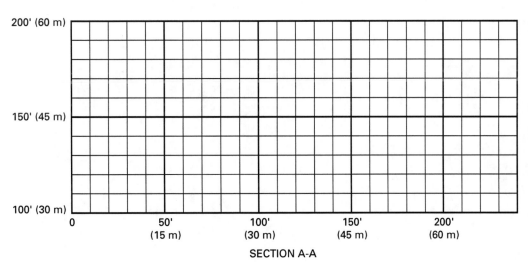

SECTION A-A

Scale: 1" = 50'-0"
(1:625 metric)

 SITE ZONING

PRACTICE EXAM: MULTIPLE CHOICE SOLUTIONS

#	Ans	#	Ans	#	Ans
1.	B	26.	B	51.	C
2.	C	27.	C	52.	C
3.	D	28.	A	53.	B
4.	B	29.	B	54.	D
5.	A	30.	A	55.	B
6.	C	31.	**14**	56.	A
7.	B	32.	C	57.	C
8.	A	33.	B	58.	B
9.	C	34.	A	59.	D
10.	D	35.	D	60.	A
11.	B	36.	C	61.	D
12.	C	37.	D	62.	B
13.	B	38.	A	63.	D
14.	D	39.	D	64.	C
15.	A, C, D, E	40.	C	65.	A, B, C, F
16.	B	41.	B	66.	D
17.	C	42.	D	67.	A
18.	B	43.	A	68.	D
19.	D	44.	C	69.	A
20.	D	45.	A	70.	A
21.	A	46.	A	71.	D
22.	A, D	47.	B	72.	C
23.	B	48.	D	73.	B
24.	C	49.	A	74.	D
25.	B	50.	A	75.	C

76. (A) ● (C) (D)
77. ● ● (C) ● (E) ●
78. ● (B) (C) (D)
79. (A) ● (C) (D)
80. (A) ● (C) (D)
81. (A) ● (C) (D)
82. (A) (B) ● (D)
83. (A) ● (C) (D)
84. (A) (B) (C) ●
85. (A) (B) (C) ●

1. The answer is B.

The first step in answering this problem is to calculate the slope between points A and B.

Grade is vertical distance over horizontal length, expressed as a percentage.

$$G = \frac{d}{L} \times 100\%$$

In U.S. units:

$$G = \frac{30 \text{ ft}}{150 \text{ ft}} \times 100\%$$

$$= 20\%$$

In SI units:

$$G = \frac{9 \text{ m}}{45 \text{ m}} \times 100\%$$

$$= 20\%$$

The slope between the two points is 20%, which would be difficult to climb and could be expensive to build on. The slope should be planted with grass to help to stabilize the soil.

Some typical slopes for various site elements are as follows.

sheet drainage	$\frac{1}{2}$% to 1%
adjacent to building, falling away from the structure	2% min.
parking areas	$1\frac{1}{2}$% to 5%
ditches	2% to 10%
ramps	5% to 8.33% max.
streets	10% max.
plant grass to stabilize soil	< 25%
plant ground cover that does not need to be mowed to stabilize soil (actual acceptable slope varies depending on soil composition)	25% to 50%
avoid slopes of 50% or greater because of the likelihood of erosion due to runoff	> 50%

2. The answer is C.

Efficiency, also called the *net-to-gross ratio*, expresses the relationship of programmed spaces to circulation, structural, and utility spaces. It is calculated by dividing the sum of the programmed spaces (the *net floor area*) by the total building area (the *gross floor area*), and is expressed as a percentage.

Buildings with heavy mechanical and circulation requirements, like hospitals, often have much lower efficiencies than buildings such as offices and retail stores. Buildings that allocate a great deal of floor space to housing the structural system (large columns, thick masonry walls, etc.) are generally less efficient than those that do not have these features. Although efficiency is determined in part by the building type, it is also dependent on the designer's skill in creating a layout with a circulation plan that occupies a minimum amount of space, so that the majority of the building's floor area can be allocated to programmed uses.

A hospital would be likely to have the lowest efficiency of the building types listed because of the space occupied by specialized mechanical systems, the wide clearances needed in hallways, and the complex circulation paths.

3. The answer is D.

The homeowners may choose to apply for a variance. A *variance* addresses situations where zoning requirements cause undue hardship for a property owner or where zoning requirements do not address a unique situation. Generally the application for a variance includes an explanation of the request and drawings depicting what will be built. The request is publicly advertised (often with a sign on the property) and then goes before a municipal board (such as a planning commission or zoning board), and comment is invited from neighbors and other interested parties. The board then makes a decision.

An *easement* allows a part of a site owned by one party to be used by another party for a specific purpose. Easements are noted on the deed and legal description of the property and may be granted for utility right-of-ways, access to an adjacent property, party walls, jointly used driveways, or conservation purposes.

A *covenant* is a restriction placed on a property by a clause in the deed. Covenants are often used to restrict the use of a property or to establish rules similar to zoning restrictions for private communities.

A *conditional use permit* allows a property to be used for a purpose that would normally not be permitted, but only if the owner fulfills certain criteria. Often, conditional use permits are granted when the proposed use is in the public interest.

4.   The answer is B.

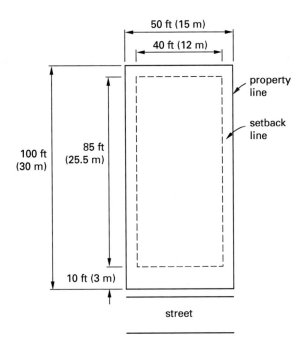

The *floor area ratio* (FAR) allowed for a specific site expresses the amount of building square footage that may be constructed relative to the total area of the site. In this case, the total area of the site is

$$A = wd$$

The floor area ratio is 2.0, so the buildable area is

$$A_{buildable} = A(\text{FAR})$$

In U.S. units:

$$A = wd = (50 \text{ ft})(100 \text{ ft}) = 5000 \text{ ft}^2$$

$$A_{buildable} = A(\text{FAR}) = (5000 \text{ ft}^2)(2.0) = 10{,}000 \text{ ft}^2$$

In SI units:

$$A = wd = (15 \text{ m})(30 \text{ m}) = 45 \text{ m}^2$$

$$A_{buildable} = A(\text{FAR}) = (450 \text{ m}^2)(2.0) = 900 \text{ m}^2$$

The three-story building, 40 ft (12 m) wide by 80 ft (24 m) deep, is the only answer choice that complies with both the setback requirements and the floor area ratio requirements.

Option A violates the site setbacks. Options C and D exceed the total buildable area permitted.

5.   The answer is A.

Greek town plans were based on a system of rectilinear blocks devoted to residential uses, with a city center containing public buildings and commerce. They included an irregular wall erected around the perimeter of the city to defend the settlement, and the size of the city was determined by the quantity of food available from surrounding areas.

Roman town plans were more regular and symmetrical than Greek plans. They were also based on a grid, with two main streets—the *cardo* and the *decananus*—intersecting at the city center. The central areas, or *fora*, featured grand buildings rather than marketplaces. Roman town plans were based on three principles: symmetry, axial connections between points of the city, and hierarchy of a primary central feature relative to subordinate accessory areas. Romans began to introduce curves to the Greek grid. Like Greek towns, the size of the Roman settlement was based on local food supplies. The locations of the settlements were influenced by local agricultural offerings, but were also chosen because they were determined to be strategic defense locations.

Medieval towns continued the tradition of enclosing a settlement within a wall, which created a clear border between the city and outlying areas. They were often built on or around the ruins of old Roman towns. They are less geometrically rigid than Roman or Greek developments because, although they were based on a grid, their developers were more likely to adjust the rectilinear plan to fit the site conditions. They are more irregular than either Greek or Roman settlements and are often clustered around a major building such as a church or cathedral. Later medieval towns often featured a star-shaped defensive wall around the settlement; each of the "points" were used as locations for lookouts and artillery.

Renaissance towns reference the Greek idea of the central cluster of public buildings and the Roman idea of a classical forum. This central gathering space often contained primary buildings and the city's marketplace. Renaissance cities were designed to be a complete and harmonious whole, considering the design of buildings, streetscapes, piazzas or courtyards, and gardens comprehensively. The appearance of many Renaissance cities is heavily influenced by Renaissance designers' appreciation of classical architecture.

6. The answer is C.

Anthropomorphism is the idea of giving human characteristics to nonhuman things. Architecture relies heavily on the proportions of the human body to determine scale, form, and the relationship of spaces and individual elements. The form and shape of parts of buildings may be influenced by the form and shape of the human body. Architects also use terms normally reserved for describing parts of the human body to describe parts of a building—the head of a door, for example.

Although the form of Casa Mila in Barcelona is very organic and sculptural, the form of the human body did not influence its design.

The Nationale-Nederlanden Building in Prague has been nicknamed "Fred and Ginger" because it resembles the forms of dancers. The caryatids at the Porch of the Maidens at the Erechtheum near the Parthenon are sculptures of women. Le Corbusier likened the ground floor columns of the Unité d'Habitation to the "strong, curvaceous thighs of a woman."

7. The answer is B.

The *comparison method*, or *market data approach*, uses information on similar-sized properties with similar amenities that are for sale in the area at the time of valuation to determine the value of a property. An investor considering the purchase of undeveloped property for commercial use would consider the prices of other similar parcels in the area, but may need to adjust the valuation to reflect other factors, such as location or access to existing utilities. If market data is available, the comparison method is the most accurate way to determine the value of all types of properties.

If market data is not available, one of the other three methods listed may be used. The *development method*, or *anticipated use method*, is used when the property may be subdivided for residential or commercial use. For example, a developer purchasing a large amount of farmland with the intention of converting it to a residential subdivision would consider the costs required for development, the physical attributes of the property and how they may affect costs (soil quality, etc.), the amount of time it will take to sell the lots, and the anticipated selling prices. The costs of development would be deducted from the projected sales prices to determine a value for the land.

The *income approach method*, also called the *residual method*, may be used for properties in areas where there is no unimproved land and no market data against which to compare. The income that will be generated by the property is estimated and compared against the cost of the site improvements. The income generated by the improvements determines the value. This method, like all valuation methods, makes the assumption that the improvements represent the *highest and best use* of the property.

The *allocation method* is used to determine the value of improved properties. This method determines the land value by deducting the value of site improvements from the total value of the property (which is equal to buildings plus land). The remainder is the value of the land.

8. The answer is A.

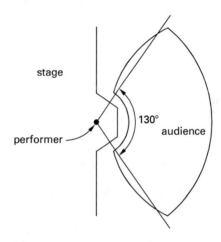

The human eye has a typical angle of vision of 130°. Therefore, a performer standing at the center of a stage will be able to make eye contact with spectators seated within this 130° range. Likewise, the spectators will be able to see the performer well as long as he or she is within their 130° range.

The *open stage* layout illustrated in option A locates the audience according to the performer's *angle of encounter* as measured from a point of command (a central point on the stage). The angle of encounter includes all of the spectators that the performer can make eye contact with while standing at this point. This arrangement would produce the greatest number of good seats, where spectators could both see and hear the performer clearly.

9. The answer is C.

A *plat* is prepared to legally define the layout of a subdivided piece of property. Plats depict new streets and rights-of-way, location and purpose of easements, lots or building sites, minimum setbacks, and any sites that are reserved for special purposes. A plat includes a statement from the owner dedicating any parts of the site that are reserved for public use. When approved, the plat becomes a part of the public land records.

A *survey* may contain much of the same information as a plat, such as location and purpose of easements, rights-of-way, and minimum setbacks, but surveys also define property boundaries and depict existing buildings and structures; utility lines on or serving the property; and remarkable natural features, such as streams, major trees, wooded areas, flood plains, and so on. The most notable difference between a survey and a plat is that a survey also includes topographical information, such as contour lines or spot elevations, that help to express the site in three dimensions.

A *master plan* may be prepared at the start of a project, during schematic design, as a tool for planning the amenities that will be included in the final plat for the property or to develop a plan for phasing the project.

A *deed* is a written document that describes the boundaries of the property and includes information about the owner and the party from whom the property was purchased.

10.   The answer is D.

The Secretary of the Interior's Standards for Rehabilitation and Guidelines for Rehabilitating Historic Buildings define the requirements for this type of work. To be eligible for federal historic preservation tax credits, these standards must be followed. The standards and additional information about historic preservation approaches are available on the National Park Service's website, www.nps.gov. A link can be found at **www.ppi2pass.com/AREresources**.

The standards advocate respecting the historic materials and character of the original building and treating them gently; repairing rather than replacing, but when replacement is necessary, replacing in kind; and recognizing that historic buildings are products of their own time and that they have evolved into their current state. When designing an addition to a historic building, the design should strive to match the historic structure in scale, materials, and character, but should not attempt to exactly replicate the historic structure; there should be a clear distinction between old and new.

There are few black and white answers when it comes to the best way to approach a historic preservation project. Each scenario must be considered individually, within the context of that specific building, and in light of the approach selected (preservation, restoration, rehabilitation, or reconstruction). In this case, the project would probably be considered rehabilitation, and the least appropriate recommendation would be to remove the trim, install furring

and insulation, replace the plaster, and reinstall the trim. The small amount of energy efficiency that might be gained through such a process would be far outweighed by the expense and the risk of destroying historic materials. In addition, the proportions of the spaces would be changed with the addition of a few inches of new wall, which would not be acceptable.

11.   The answer is B.

Permanent seeding and landscaping of a site is a stabilization measure that can prevent erosion. As stormwater runoff travels over the site, the root stuctures of grasses and other plantings can help prevent the runoff from washing the soil away.

The three other methods listed are structural control techniques. They will not prevent erosion, but they will contain the sediment and prevent it from traveling into local rivers, lakes, or streams. An *earth dyke* is a mound of soil that diverts water to a *sediment trap*, or pond, where sediment is allowed to settle out of the water. A *silt fence* acts as a filter for water flowing across the site and traps the sediment before it can be washed into a nearby body of water.

12.   The answer is C.

Brunelleschi's dome at Florence Cathedral, built in the 1420s, was the first to be constructed without centering. *Centering* is wooden framework erected to support the masonry comprising the dome before it is complete. Because the drum at Florence Cathedral was constructed before the dome was designed and was very large, the use of centering was not possible. Brunelleschi developed a design for a double-shell, pointed dome with a ribbed structure infilled with lightweight materials.

The Pantheon is believed to have been built around A.D. 118 to 128. Although the base of the dome at the Pantheon was constructed using a corbeling technique, it is believed that the hemispherical portion of the coffered concrete dome was constructed with centering. The dome of St. Peter's Basilica in Rome was constructed more than 100 years after Florence Cathedral and, like Brunelleschi's dome, is slightly pointed. The U.S. Capitol dome was built in the 1800s and is made of cast iron rather than masonry.

13.   The answer is B.

Condominium is a form of ownership in which a buyer obtains absolute title to a portion of a structure. It can be used for either residential or commercial applications.

Usually, a condominium owner has common tenancy of the land, parking areas and access roads, and site improvements (pools, tennis courts, etc.) associated with the property. Often fees are assessed to condominium owners to cover the expenses of maintaining these common areas. Owners can sell their properties and are responsible for paying their own property taxes.

Fee simple means that the owner has absolute title to the property and may sell it to another person, if desired.

A *leasehold* entitles the lessee to the use of the property for a specified period of time, during which the lessee pays rent. The lessee may not sell the property, but may sell the right to occupy the property, which is called a *sublease*.

Cooperative ownership means that the owner does not hold the title to the property, but owns a share of a corporation that owns the property. In return, the stockholder may occupy a portion of the property. The person may sell their stock to another individual or company, but the corporation always retains full ownership of the building and land.

14.   The answer is D.

Project relationships between owners, architects, and contractors may be based on the idea of *partnering*. Partnering is not a contractual relationship, but is an agreement between the parties to work together toward the common goal of constructing a building. The concept is based on eliminating the adversarial relationship that may develop between project participants. The partnering agreement is a commitment to one another to work together and respect the knowledge each party brings to the project. It can potentially result in a lower cost to the owner, a shorter construction period, and less paperwork for everyone, and it may reduce the number of project disputes.

A partnering agreement may or may not be a written document; AIA *Best Practices* recommends using a *partnering charter*, developed during a workshop facilitated by someone not involved with the project in which all team members participate, that outlines the responsibilities and goals of the team. Or, the agreement can be as simple as a discussion over lunch or a handshake on the golf course between companies with a long history of working together.

The American Arbitration Association established a task force to study partnering in 1995. The conclusions reached by the committee provide a good explanation of partnering. A link to these conclusions may be found at **www.ppi2pass.com/AREresources**.

15.   The answer is A, D, and E.

An *adjacency* or *affinity matrix* is a way of graphically representing which spaces should be adjacent to one another. This simple diagram is read by following the lines representing the spaces to the box at which they meet. If there is a closed dot in the box, the rooms should be adjacent to one another. If the dot is open, the spaces have some relationship but need not be adjacent.

16.   The answer is B.

Broadacre City was a concept explored by Frank Lloyd Wright in his 1932 book, *The Disappearing City*. This treatise was written in the middle of the Great Depression, long before the post-war explosion of the suburbs in the United States.

Wright argued that the idea of the urban center was no longer relevant. Under the Broadacre City plan, each American family would be given an acre (4000 m^2) of land from the federal land reserves on which they would build a home and grow their own food.

The original concept for Broadacre City and Wright's further refinement of his ideas in writings such as *The Living City*, published in 1958, explained that technologies such as the car, radio, telephone, telegraph, and standardized production would shape the new city. Wright's drawings and models of Broadacre City showed the area filled with his designs, including Usonian houses. The scheme depended almost exclusively on use of the private automobile for transportation and provided very little accommodation for pedestrian needs or public transportation.

17.   The answer is C.

A *brownfield* is a property where redevelopment or reuse may be complicated by the presence of contaminants. These properties may have once been factories, gas stations, quarries, armories, or other types of buildings where chemicals or pollutants were stored. These sites generally have some existing infrastructure.

From a sustainability standpoint, the redevelopment of a property is far preferable to development of a site that has not been previously altered (which is called a *greenfield*). Developing a brownfield site requires cleaning up the contamination through either bioremediation, in situ (on-site) remediation, or off-site procedures. As an alternative, the hazardous materials may remain on site and be contained in such a way that they will not come in contact with humans.

Federal tax credits and incentive programs are in place to encourage the use of brownfield sites rather than greenfields. LEED points are awarded for the rehabilitation of a brownfield. For more information, refer to the Environmental Protection Agency's webpage on brownfields and land revitalization. A link to the page can be found at **www.ppi2pass.com/AREresources**.

18.   The answer is B.

Bridging is a specific approach to the design-build model of project delivery that allows an owner to secure an early fixed price and take advantage of the contractor's knowledge of construction methods and materials and relationships with suppliers. Bridging allows an owner to establish which things he or she wants to control, gives responsibility for details of construction to the contractor, and permits the owner to obtain the advice and participation of an architect.

The primary advantages of bridging are that

- a contract price can be obtained more quickly and with a lower up-front cost than with a design-bid-build approach

- the contractor bears sole responsibility for the product of construction with the benefit of an architect's involvement

- bridging is more cost effective

First, the project is defined by an architect and/or project manager, sometimes called the "criteria architect" or "bridging consultant," who prepares drawings similar to the traditional product of the design development phase. These are referred to as the *contract documents*. The consultant obtains bids from prequalified design-build contractors, and the contract is awarded to the low bidder. Then, the design-build contractor develops the construction documents and is the Architect of Record for the project. The owner's architect/project manager reviews the construction documents to determine conformance with the original contract documents.

The contractor then builds the facility. The architect/project manager administers the contract for construction. The construction documents are used for construction and permitting, but the contract between the owner and contractor is based on the contract documents.

A link to an essay explaining bridging may be found at **www.ppi2pass.com/AREresources**.

19.   The answer is D.

When preparing cost opinions, it is a good idea to tack on a contingency allowance to provide for unforeseen conditions. The allowance usually varies from 5% to 20% (or more) of the estimated construction cost. The earlier the stage of the project, the higher the contingency should be. For example, a cost opinion prepared during the schematic design phase based on unit costs would have a much higher contingency factor than one prepared just before the project goes to bid, when the quantities and materials are better defined. In this problem, the highest contingency allowance should be tacked onto the cost opinion prepared during programming for the elementary school, as this project has the highest level of uncertainty.

20.   The answer is D.

The National Environmental Policy Act of 1969 requires all "major federal actions" to submit an *environmental impact statement* describing the project and analyzing its potential impact on the environment. This requirement applies to all projects receiving federal funding or licensing. Environmental impact statements (EIS) are submitted to the Council on Environmental Quality, which advises the President on environmental development issues. The EIS is then submitted to the Environmental Protection Agency.

Environmental impact statements must comply with the *rule of reason*, meaning that if a reasonable person would consider an alternative to be viable, then that alternative must be included. One of the alternatives that must always be included is the option of not undertaking the project.

Basic information on environmental impact statements may be found in the Ohio State University Cooperative Extension Fact Sheet CDFS-188, *Environmental Impact Statements*, at **www.ppi2pass.com/AREresources**, and on the Environmental Protection Agency's website, www.epa.gov.

21.   The answer is A.

A *radial* organizational pattern best facilitates social interaction, because all inhabitants of a building pass through a central core to move to other spaces. This pattern is popular in secondary school design, where wings—a science wing, a humanities wing, the industrial arts shops, and so on—branch off from a central space housing common amenities like the library.

An *axial* pattern, option B, connects two major spaces on the main axis with secondary paths branching off from either side. This organizational pattern is often used for shopping malls.

Most American cities are based on the *grid* pattern (option C). This strategy is easy to expand and easy to interpret, even for a first-time visitor. It can become monotonous, though, unless portions of the city or building break from the grid to form areas of surprise and complexity.

A *precinctual* pattern (option D) works well for buildings that house a number of dispersed activities. This organizational technique could be used for an office building housing several distinct companies. Advantages of this strategy are flexibility, efficiency, and economy.

22. The answer is A and D.

If the critical path is shortened, direct costs will increase. A shorter construction period requires more equipment and more worker-hours to accomplish the same amount of work in a reduced amount of time. As the labor force is increased or work hours are extended, workers tend to become less efficient and supervision becomes more difficult. Therefore, quality control levels often decrease, because laborers trying to work quickly are likely to make more errors.

Overhead costs decrease when a schedule is shortened. Each day that the contractor must rent an office trailer, pay a superintendent's salary, or cover other overhead expenses costs a fixed amount of money. If the construction period is shortened, the contractor incurs fewer expenses and the total overhead decreases. Activities on float paths may have to be completed more quickly to finish a project on time, but a change in the critical path schedule would not delay these tasks.

23. The answer is B.

An *affirmative covenant* commits a buyer to performing a specific duty in the future. By purchasing the grocery store, the owner agrees to maintain the garden and keep it available for public use. This type of covenant runs with the land, so the seating area will be open to the public in perpetuity.

A *conditional covenant* states that if the restrictions prescribed in the deed are not followed, the title to the land will revert to the original grantor or his or her heirs. A *conditional use permit* provides permission from a zoning board to use a property for a special purpose; the purpose may not comply with the zoning restrictions in force in that area, but the project is permitted because the use serves the public (such as a hospital in a residential neighborhood).

There is no clause in such a deed known as a *prescriptive covenant*.

24. The answer is C.

Payroll taxes are considered to be a part of labor costs.

General overhead costs are those expenses that a contractor cannot attribute directly to a project. Overhead expenses include things like rent and utilities, advertising, office supplies, general legal expenses, and staff wages.

Project overhead costs can be charged to a specific project, but they exclude labor, materials, and equipment. Overhead costs could include bonds and insurance, temporary facilities, permits, and transportation related to the project, as well as other expenses the contractor may incur in the course of the work.

Total overhead costs vary from 5% to 20% of project costs. Overhead expenses are generally related to the size of the contractor's operation. For example, a general contractor working from his home, advertising through word of mouth, and coordinating the work through subcontractors rather than employing his own forces would have much lower overhead than a large construction company with hundreds of employees, large offices in a downtown highrise, and an advertising campaign that makes their firm a household word.

25. The answer is B.

Eminent domain is the right of a government to acquire private property for a use that is determined to be in the public interest. It is granted by the Fifth Amendment to the U.S. Constitution, which states, "…nor shall private property be taken for public use, without just compensation." The power of eminent domain may be transferred to a private company, such as a utility company, railroad, port authority, and so on, when that entity is working on a project that is determined to serve the public interest. The U.S. Supreme Courts decision in *Kelo v. City of New London* determined that the power of eminent domain may be also used by a private, for-profit company when the project serves the public interest by promoting economic development.

Eminent domain laws are intended to allow public projects to move forward while fairly compensating private property owners for their property and any other damages, such as relocation expenses. This process is sometimes referred to as *condemnation*.

A condemnor must be authorized by statute or ordinance to use the power of eminent domain for a specific purpose.

The condemnor must first make an offer to buy the property from the property owner. If they cannot agree, eminent domain proceedings may be initiated, where the condemnor will be required to prove that the property is to be acquired for a public purpose. If the judge agrees that use of eminent domain is appropriate, hearings begin to determine the fair market value of the property. The judge may appoint a panel of "condemnation commissioners" who determine the fair market value or, if this is not satisfactory to either party, he or she may appoint a jury to determine the award. The property owner is then paid the determined fair market value plus any other damages the court deems appropriate.

26.   The answer is B.

Traditionally, real estate laws were based on the Latin phrase *cuius est solum, ejus est usque ad caelum et ad inferos*, which means "whomever owns the land shall own the earth to its center and up to the heavens." Modern interpretations of land rights are a bit more complicated.

Air rights permit a party to use the open space above land or an existing structure. Air rights can be sold or transferred to another party. For example, in Boston, space above the Massachusetts Turnpike can be leased for development of buildings and parks constructed on massive platforms. Christ Church in New York City sold its air rights for $430 per square foot to developers who will "transfer" the unused vertical space to another building, so that structure can be built higher than zoning ordinances would normally allow. Air rights do not give a property owner the right to prohibit aircraft from entering that space; in the United States, the Federal Aviation Administration controls where aircraft can and cannot fly, not individual property owners.

Riparian rights allow property owners whose lots abut a body of water the right to make use of that resource. *Littoral rights* are similar to riparian rights but apply to areas along the shores of oceans and navigable lakes. *Subsurface rights* pertain to oil, coal, and other minerals found beneath the surface of the land.

27.   The answer is C.
Baroque cities are characterized by their long vistas linking important points within the city and by their comprehensive approach to planning both grand public spaces and residential areas. They were heavily influenced by the ideas expressed at Versailles and by other work of French landscape architects.

Sir Christopher Wren's plan for London's redevelopment after the Great Fire, drafted in 1666, used these principals, but was never constructed as drawn. Baron Georges-Eugène Haussman's plan for modern Paris (1853 to 1869) created sweeping boulevards capped by monuments and public parks in the Baroque tradition. In 1791, Pierre-Charles L'Enfant proposed a plan for Washington, D.C., that included diagonal avenues radiating from the U.S. Capitol and the White House, superimposed over a grid system.

New York City was not designed in the Baroque manner. It is laid out according to a grid plan, mandated by the Commissioners' Plan of 1811, which disregarded topography entirely and superimposed a rectilinear grid over the majority of the island of Manhattan. (Central Park was not a part of the original plan for New York. In 1853, Frederick Law Olmstead and Calvert Vaux were commissioned to develop a plan for the park, which would interrupt the grid and bring greenspace into the city.)

28. The answer is A.

A *building footprint* is determined by analyzing the interaction of three variables. The first variable is the *total gross area*, which is the sum of the programmed spaces plus circulation and service spaces.

The second variable is the *number of floors*, which is generally determined by the program, zoning requirements, and buildable area of the site. For example, a building with a program of 90,000 ft^2 (8370 m^2) could be constructed as a sprawling, one-story structure, or the functions could be stacked into a structure with multiple floors. A compact, multilevel structure tends to be more economical in terms of utility distribution and long-term maintenance and is a better strategy for preserving the natural characteristics of a previously undeveloped site; however, it may cost more to construct.

The third variable for determining a building footprint is the *building configuration*. For example, the first floor of a building may have more square footage than each of the upper floors, so the building footprint would be different from the average floor area.

A *use group* is a classification for a building based on the type of occupancy and is prescribed by the local code.

29. The answer is B.

To determine if a site and its potential use are compatible, an architect and client must first develop a *program*, a list of spaces needed in the building and their approximate sizes. This document will serve as the "instruction manual" for the project. The architect in this scenario should work with the client to develop this document and compare it against the existing space to see if the new use is compatible with the old structure. If it is determined to be a good fit, the process of site analysis can move forward. After that it will be important to study code issues, parking requirements, environmental concerns, and the historic value of the property to determine if the project is architecturally feasible. Simultaneously, the client should be developing the project *pro forma*, which examines the financial feasibility of the project. If the results of both studies indicate that the project should go ahead, the architect may begin to prepare schematic design concepts for the renovation.

30. The answer is A.

Designing a taller building with a smaller footprint to minimize site disturbance is the best approach to development on a previously undisturbed, or *greenfield*, site. A smaller footprint results in less area of impervious surfaces (which minimizes runoff) and limits the disturbance to existing landscaping and wildlife habitats. A smaller footprint generally results in a more energy- and resource-efficient building as well, with lower long-term maintenance costs.

31. The answer is 14.

The *critical path* is the path that takes the most amount of time to complete. In this diagram, the critical path is 1-2-3-4-5-6, and it will take 14 days to complete these activities.

32. The answer is C.

As the floor area of the building increases, the cost per unit of area decreases. This decrease is attributable to better perimeter-to-floor area ratios (as mentioned in option A; the exterior envelope is a costly building component) and more efficient utilization of the most expensive elements of the building, such as the HVAC system and elevators. The contractor can also capitalize on *economies of scale*, which means that the more materials purchased, the better the deal.

Larger buildings tend to have lower unit costs. An exception is tall buildings: above six stories or so, costs per square foot tend to increase due to the need for elevators, additional fire protection measures, and specialized structural systems. As floor-to-floor heights increase, so do unit costs; this may be attributed to a need to use nonstandard building materials. In wood frame construction, for example, exceeding an 8 ft (2.4 m) ceiling height requires that sheets of gypsum board must be cut to fit.

In addition to design factors mentioned, the cost per unit may also be affected by the length of the construction period, unusual contractual requirements, and the quality of the materials specified.

33. The answer is B.

The prescribed height of a classical column is a multiple of the diameter. Historically, Doric columns were the fattest, with a ratio of $4^1/_2{:}1$ or $5^1/_2{:}1$. Ionic columns were more slender, with a diameter-to-height ratio of 9:1 or 10:1. The Corinthian order, which is a variation of the Ionic, had similar proportions.

34. The answer is A.

An architect's opinion of the cost of the work would only include the project as designed by the architect and her consultants. *Hard costs* are the costs of labor and materials. The contractor's overhead and profit allowances would be included as well because that is a part of the expense of constructing the building. Also, contingency allowances should be included, particularly in early opinions, to cover design contingencies, unforeseen conditions, inflation, and potential changes in the marketplace.

The architect's estimate would not include professional fees (neither the architect's nor her consultants or those of any consultants the owner chooses to hire independently) and other project costs, such as the cost of the land, costs related to financing, legal expenses, or other items that are not a part of the cost of the architect's work. These items are more appropriately included in the project budget, which would be developed by the owner.

35. The answer is D.

The amount of retainage at substantial completion frequently is comparable to the contractor's profit for the job—anywhere from 5% to 20%; commonly about 10%. Therefore, the contractor is often anxious to establish a substantial completion date and resolve any outstanding punch list items or other unresolved issues expeditiously, so that they may receive final payment.

36.   The answer is C.

Efficiency is the ratio of net area to gross area and is always a number between zero and one. A building's program and design decisions made in the initial planning stages can have a great impact on a building's efficiency. Deciding to build a new building designed specifically to meet the program requirements generally leads to a more efficient building than retrofitting an existing building to meet new needs. The site has an effect as well; sites with lots of open space and gentle grades can help to increase building efficiency. Consultants' choices can also have a significant impact on efficiency; for example, placing mechanical units on the roof rather than in an interior mechanical room can help to increase efficiency. Furthermore, programs that require large rooms, specify flexible requirements regarding adjacencies and/or windows, and have a low population as defined by the code (requiring smaller means of egress) tend to be more efficient. A designer can further increase the efficiency of a building by limiting the design to one story with a central core and by using double-loaded corridors.

37. The answer is D.

A *core* is the focus of a district that may be perceived as a symbol of that part of the city. The core is often located at the junction of primary paths, or could be an element or feature that influences the rest of the area. For example, a core might be a large open air market, a baseball stadium, or a street with lots of shops and restaurants. A core attracts people to the area, is served by the major transportation paths, and is the first image that most people associate with that part of the city.

The Image of the City discusses the legibility of cities and ways to "read" them. It also focuses on the mental images of cities that people use to find their way. There are five elements in Lynch's city; in Lynch's words, these are

- *paths*: "channels along which the observer customarily, occasionally, or potentially moves"

- *edges*: "linear elements not used or considered paths by the observer"

- *districts*: "sections of the city which the observer mentally enters 'inside of' and which are recognizable as having some common, identifying character"

- *nodes*: "points, the strategic spots in a city into which an observer can enter, and which are the intensive foci to and from which he is traveling"

- *landmarks*: "another type of point reference, but in this case, the observer does not enter within them, they are external"

38.   The answer is A.

The forest/woodlands area would be the most suitable area for development on this site. Of the areas identified, the forest/woodland is the most tolerant to human use at appropriate densities and when developed in a way that retains many of the inherent characteristics of the land.

Design with Nature identifies eight categories of open space and lists them in order of the value of their natural processes and their degree of intolerance to development. The inverse of the list ranks the sites in order of their suitability for development. From least tolerant of development to most tolerant, these areas are

- surface water

- marshes

- floodplains

- aquifer recharge areas

- aquifers

- steep slopes

- forests and woodlands

- flat land excluding prime agricultural land

39.   The answer is D.

Sitecast concrete one-way solid slab systems allow the designer to expose the structural system while maintaining a high fire-resistance rating. Construction time can be minimized with this system by designing repetitive elements so formwork can be reused. The system can be used with either bearing walls (less expensive, good for multiple repetitive elements) or beams and girders (more expensive, but more flexible for longer spans or greater loads).

Neither wood platform framing nor either type of steel framing would permit the structure to be exposed and maintain required fire ratings. While the steel frame with rigid connections may help to reduce construction time, neither the light-gauge steel framing system nor the wood platform frame would help to speed up construction of a four-story building.

40.   **The answer is C.**

Room data sheets are questionnaires completed by end users or by programming team members based on interviews with end users of the spaces within a building. They are designed to help the programmer better understand the uses of the space, the people and things that the space is required to house (occupants, furniture, and equipment), unique finish or construction requirements, and any special mechanical, electrical, or acoustical requirements. The results of the surveys are then compiled into a document that helps the programmer to determine the appropriate area and location of each space within a building based on the established criteria.

Room data sheets are most effective for programming studies of buildings with many varying types of spaces. However, for buildings with lots of repetitive spaces or hard-to-define end users, they are not very helpful. Therefore, the best application of room data sheets listed is the high school, because the function and use of the rooms may vary greatly and teachers and administrators could be interviewed about the needs of each space to determine appropriate sizes and relationships.

41.   **The answer is B.**

A *100-year flood* is the maximum flood level with a 1% probability of occurring within a given year. This is the standard used by the National Flood Insurance Program for determining risk to a specific property and specifying which properties are required to have flood insurance to receive federally backed financing. Special hazard flood areas are shown on flood insurance risk maps, and properties within the boundaries must comply with special requirements for design and construction, particularly requirements for siting, lowest building elevations, and acceptable materials and construction methods.

The Federal Emergency Management Agency publishes a series of fact sheets discussing construction within flood-prone areas and along the coast, addressing both flooding and high winds. A link to them may be found at **www.ppi2pass.com/AREresources**.

42.   **The answer is D.**

Although any of the items mentioned could be a part of an architect-consultant agreement, none of them is required. The agreement can be written (which is recommended) or oral, and should outline what is expected of each party. Two major issues should be addressed: passing through rights and responsibilities of the architect to the consultant, and sharing risks and rewards. The agreement should also address compensation.

Passing through responsibility and rights is often accomplished by incorporating the owner-architect agreement. AIA Document C401, *Standard Form of Agreement Between Architect and Consultant*, is coordinated with AIA Document B101 to accomplish this. If the AIA documents are not used, the architect should ensure that the consultant is aware of his or her duties in all phases of the project. The agreement should also establish responsibilities such as internal coordination, revisions on request of the architect, cost estimating, assistance with the bidding process, review of shop drawings, and site visits.

When undertaking a project, an architect assumes a certain amount of risk. This risk is appropriately shared with the consultant as a member of the project team, and the architect may require provisions addressing this risk to be a part of the agreement. For example, the architect can be held liable if consultant's duties are not performed with reasonable care; therefore, the architect may decide that it is prudent for the consultant to carry liability insurance.

43.   **The answer is A.**

A *milestone chart* would be appropriate for this project schedule. Milestone charts are best for scheduling small projects with few participants. They consist of a list of deadlines and assignment of responsibility for each task. With only three people directly involved with this project, this type of schedule would be a good way to set goals and keep the project on track.

Bar charts, or *Gantt charts*, show both start and finish dates and work well for larger architectural projects. *CPM*, or the *critical path method*, shows complex interrelationships between tasks. This scheduling method can be used for extremely large architectural projects, but more commonly is used by contractors to coordinate construction.

44.   The answer is C.

The *Modulor* system of proportioning uses the human body as a starting point and is loosely based on the golden section.

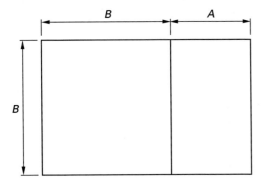

The *golden section* is based purely on mathematics. It is defined as the division of a line so that the lesser portion is to the greater as the greater is to the whole, or

$$\frac{B}{A} = \frac{A + B}{B}$$

In the preceding figure, the large rectangle is divided into a square and a small rectangle. If the sides of the large rectangle ($A + B$ and B) are in the ratio of the golden section, then so are the sides of the small rectangle (B and A). The ratio B/A is known as ϕ and is equal to about 1.618.

In antiquity through today, the classical orders have been based on the relationship of the diameter of the column to the height and sizes of other building elements.

The *ken* is a unit of measurement in Japanese culture based on the size of a floor mat and is used repetitively to organize floor plans and elevations.

45.   The answer is A.

Placing the parking areas under the building makes good sense in terms of sustainability because it disrupts less of the site and minimizes areas of imperviousness, but in terms of safety and security it could be difficult to protect the building from vehicle bombs.

Constructed wetlands are used to process wastewater, but they could also serve as an additional barrier to vehicular and pedestrian access to the building depending on where they are placed on the site. Integrated building automation and control systems help ensure that the mechanical systems in the building are operating efficiently; they can also be used to detect contaminants in the building. Trombe walls are used for passive solar heating, but their mass could also help the building resist a bomb impact.

46.   The answer is A.

Construction management at risk is a project delivery approach that employs a construction manager to oversee the project; this method is often used for fast-track construction, where the design and construction phases may overlap.

The architect is hired by the owner and begins the project. The construction manager is hired by the owner during the design phase and advises the owner on issues of scheduling, constructability, and cost. At some point, the construction manager usually offers the owner a guaranteed maximum price and, if the price is accepted, becomes the general contractor. The term "at risk" is used because the construction manager takes on the risk of performance. The construction manager may then subcontract the work to other contractors to complete construction.

A link to an essay on the construction management at risk method of project delivery can be found at **www.ppi2pass.com/AREresources**.

47.   The answer is B.

Cost evaluations performed during the programming stage often compare a proposed project to a model project of similar size and scope. A *premium* is something that will add cost to a project in comparison to the model. Examples of premiums are short construction periods, unusual contract provisions (extra insurance, liquidated damages, etc.), challenging site conditions, and nonstandard programmatic elements or client requirements, such as the need to use prevailing wage rates or union labor.

Cost evaluation during programming is difficult because there are so many unknowns. Listing potential premiums helps the architect and owner to get a feel for how much the unknowns or unique conditions may add to the cost of the project. As the project progresses, it is necessary to reevaluate the costs attributed to the premiums as the design, materials, and conditions under which the project will be constructed become more defined.

48.   The answer is D.

Trees can have a variety of effects on the microclimate of a site. The cluster of trees that are all roughly the same height would be a more effective windbreak than any of the other configurations shown. When placed correctly to reduce the amount of winter wind reaching the structure, a windbreak such as this can create a more comfortable microclimate and reduce heating costs.

49.   The answer is A.

A dashed line represents an existing contour line. A solid contour line shows an area where the earth is to be manipulated. In both cases, the elevation is noted on the high side of the contour.

A line composed of long dashes with two short dashes in between usually represents a property line. A line comprised of dashes and Xs may be used to represent fencing.

50.   The answer is A.

Unit prices are proposed by the contractor with her bid and are agreed on in Article 4.3 of AIA Document A101.

51.   The answer is C.

The primary advantage to the fast-track method of project delivery is the ability to overlap the design and construction phases to complete a project more quickly. This method can be used in cases where an owner must occupy a new facility within a certain period of time or when other costs are rising rapidly, such as labor rates, material costs, or interest rates. Fast-tracking a project usually involves hiring a design-build firm or breaking the project into several prime contracts and awarding them sequentially as construction progresses.

The AIA/American General Contractors Association publication *Primer on Project Delivery* addresses methods of providing design and construction services. Links to it and an essay on project delivery strategy can be found at **www.ppi2pass.com/AREresources.**

52.   The answer is C.

Defensible space is a concept originally explored by Oscar Newman in the 1970s. Through a partnership with the Department of Housing and Urban Development, Newman expanded and updated his ideas in a book called *Creating Defensible Space*, which can be downloaded for free from www.defensiblespace.com.

Newman's work was sparked by the demise of Pruitt-Igoe, a housing complex in St. Louis, Missouri, that was planned according to the most contemporary architectural thinking but was a disaster in terms of vandalism and crime. The complex was imploded about 10 years after it was constructed. The book's thesis is that designing a space that allows residents a sense of ownership and control (unlike Pruitt-Igoe) leads to an environment that people care about and will work to maintain and protect. In his book, written

in cooperation with HUD, Newman examines these ideas through case studies of three projects.

In low- to moderate-income housing facilities, large, public spaces (such as common rooms or elevator lobbies) feel anonymous and are more likely to be vandalized. Newman's research indicates that the crime rate in a housing project increases as the number of units per entry (building height) increases and as the size of the building project increases. In contrast, a few families sharing a common entry vestibule creates a semiprivate space that those occupants can monitor. When residents have the ability to oversee the street, their feelings of association with the neighborhood, and thus of "neighbors looking out for one another," are further increased.

53.   The answer is B.

An *infiltration basin* is a pond that temporarily collects water and allows it to be released only through absorption into the earth. This helps to recharge the groundwater on the site rather than dumping it into a storm sewer, as a *catch basin* does.

A *bioswale* is a grassy sloped ditch that filters the storm runoff as it is directed away from a building or paved area. It allows the water to seep into the ground and also helps to recharge aquifers.

A *cistern* is a tank for collecting and storing water. It is often used with rainwater harvest systems that capture and store rainwater for use in irrigation or nonpotable building functions, such as flushing toilets.

54.   The answer is D.

A *public enterprise revenue bond* is issued to fund a public project that will produce revenue; the bond is repaid with the money generated by the facility. This type of bond may be issued to finance a project like an airport, a hospital, or a stadium.

A *general obligation bond* is used to fund public projects that will not produce revenue. These are often used to finance schools, public libraries, or municipal buildings. The bond is repaid through property, or *ad valorem*, taxes. General obligation bond measures must be approved by voters in the jurisdiction.

Development impact fees are charged to developers to pay for public improvements that are necessary because of the development. Fees may be assessed to cover the costs of road improvements, utility extensions, or other upgrades required for the private development project that must be provided by the municipality.

55. The answer is B.

A school district could be considered a catchment area for a region's educational facilities. Master planning for a school district would begin with a study of the population of the area and how many children are living within the boundaries of the district. The schools could then be planned to accommodate the children and allow for future growth or decline, depending on population trends in the area.

56.   The answer is A.

The strategies listed would be most appropriate for a cool climate. A good example of a building type designed around these strategies is the New England saltbox, which has a blank north elevation and steep overhang to minimize the size of the wall, a taller south elevation, a tight, spare form, an economical design, and a dark shingled exterior. Cool climates in the United States are found in northern New England, the northern Midwest, the Rocky Mountains, and Alaska.

57.   The answer is C.

Efficiency expresses the ratio of net assignable area, or programmed space, to the gross area of the building.

$$\text{efficiency} = \frac{\text{net area}}{\text{gross area}}$$

$$\text{gross area} = \frac{\text{net area}}{\text{efficiency}}$$

In U.S. units:

$$\text{gross area} = \frac{32{,}000 \text{ ft}^2}{0.75}$$
$$= 42{,}667 \text{ ft}^2$$

In SI units:

$$\text{gross area} = \frac{3000 \text{ m}^2}{0.75}$$
$$= 4000 \text{ m}^2$$

58.   The answer is B.

Restoration focuses on the most important time period in the life of a structure. In this case, the most significant time was the Battle of Gettysburg, July 1 through 3, 1863. Therefore, any additions built at other times could be removed. The materials and character of the original structure should be repaired.

Rehabilitation is often used when the property is being converted to a use other than its historical function. It allows more flexibility in the materials and methods of construction that can be used to repair the building, as long as the historic character of the building is maintained.

Reconstruction is the process of rebuilding a lost structure based on historical documentation. One of the most familiar examples of this approach is the buildings and environs at Colonial Williamsburg.

Preservation is the most historically accurate approach. It maintains additions made over time and chronicles the history of the building through the modifications.

59.   The answer is D.

A *behavior setting* is the "stage" for an event that occurs at a particular place on a regular schedule. The activities that happen within the behavior setting are definable, and the physical environmental facilitates that activity. Every building is designed around a sequence of behavior settings, whether that setting is a family's morning routine in their home, a classroom setting in a school, or an operating room in a hospital. The actions of the inhabitants can be analyzed to discover the best way for the physical environment to facilitate their activities.

60.   The answer is A.

The Secretary of the Interior's Standards for Rehabilitation offer guidelines for treatment of historic properties. The solution to Prob. 58 discusses the four acceptable approaches. The standards can be found on the National Park Service website, or a current link can be found at **www.ppi2pass.com/AREresources**.

61.   The answer is D.

The solution to Prob. 52 discusses the genesis and principles of Oscar Newman's idea of defensible space. The case studies cited in his book describe some of the techniques used to help create a sense of pride of ownership in a neighborhood.

In Dayton, Ohio, mini-neighborhoods were created through the use of gated streets. However, as Newman pointed out, gated streets alone are insufficient; successfully implementing the principles of defensible space requires stricter enforcement of building codes (including attaching criminal charges for noncompliance), help for new homeowners to finance and maintain their properties, and community programs designed to facilitate interaction among neighbors.

At Clason Point in New York City, Newman describes a row house project where the aesthetics of the community contributed to its demise: "temporary" concrete block buildings outfitted with vandal-resistant materials and separated by open spaces that were perceived as dangerous. Newman and the planners introduced barriers such as curbs and fences to better define private and semiprivate spaces, limited and widened pedestrian walkways to allow for better visibility and supervision, and refaced existing structures with more "residential" materials that the residents helped to choose. They also allocated a portion of the common grounds to each family and encouraged them to grow grass in order to take ownership of the space outside their homes.

In Yonkers, New York, implementing defensible space principles involved scattering factory-built row houses on a number of sites throughout the city, rather than clustering the low-income residents in a high-rise.

62. The answer is B.

An *area of refuge*, sometimes called an *area of rescue assistance*, is a space that can serve as a temporary shelter for building inhabitants as they evacuate during a fire. It is primarily designed for occupants who cannot use stairways, and it provides a protected place for them to wait until help can arrive.

An area of refuge must be located on the same floor level but may be in a different part of the building from the area that it serves. According to the *International Building Code*, it must accommodate one wheelchair space (30 in × 42 in; 760 mm × 1065 mm) for each 200 occupants or portion thereof. The area of refuge must be separated with a smoke barrier, and two-way communications must be provided so that an inhabitant can communicate with emergency personnel. Instructions must also be provided that explain escape procedures and how to use the communications system.

63. The answer is D.

An *arterial* connects an *expressway*, such as an interstate, to a street serving a residential area, called a *collector-distributor*. The collector-distributor then connects to *local access roads* within the neighborhood.

Access to expressways is often restricted to entrance and exit ramps to allow traffic to move faster and unimpeded. Arterials are usually two lanes in each direction, and no parking is permitted on the street. They generally are controlled by traffic lights. Sometimes arterials are populated with restaurants and shopping areas.

Collector-distributors may be one lane in each direction, and parking may be permitted on the street at certain times of the day. They also are often controlled by traffic lights.

Local access streets are usually only one lane in each direction or may be one way, and they are generally controlled by stop signs. They may take the form of loops or cul-de-sacs. Generally, on-street parking is unrestricted.

64. The answer is C.

Budget prices are normally escalated to reflect the anticipated price at the midpoint of construction.

65. The answer is A, B, C, and F.

The allowable height of a building is determined by the use group and type of construction and may be increased if a fire-suppression system or adequate street frontage is provided. Local zoning ordinances may also restrict the height of a structure.

66. The answer is D.

An outside stairway with solid treads may be counted as a required exit. It must comply with the fire-resistance requirements of an interior stair and, in some climates, must be covered with a roof to protect it from snow.

Escalators, elevators, and fire escapes are not permitted to be counted as required exits.

67. The answer is A.

Where possible, buildings should not penetrate the water table. Sites where the water table is less than 6 ft (1.8 m) below the surface may require special techniques during excavation.

68.   **The answer is D.**

Specifying materials with low albedo and high conductivity
will help to moderate the microclimate. *Albedo* is a measurement of a material's solar reflectance: the higher the
number, the more reflective the surface. *Conductivity* measures the speed with which heat travels through a material.

Examples of materials with low albedo are traditional concrete and dark-colored gravel. Materials with high conductivity include sand and soil.

69.   **The answer is A.**

Article 1 of AIA Document B101 allows incorporation of the
project program as a part of the initial information, and
Sec. 5.1 requires the owner to furnish this information.

The owner may choose to hire an architect to perform a
programming study or to coordinate this process; these
would be considered changes to the architect's services for
which additional compensation could be requested.

70.   **The answer is A.**

Minimum parking requirements for a site are generally
determined by a local zoning ordinance. In the absence of
such an ordinance, they may be determined by the program
(one space for every two seats in a movie theater, for example). If the owner wishes to provide more parking than is
required by the zoning ordinance, the quantity of the additional parking spaces is at his or her discretion provided
that the site will accommodate them. The *ADA/ABA Guidelines* require that a percentage of the parking spaces provided be accessible, but they do not establish overall
parking requirements.

71.   **The answer is D.**

Joint ventures are agreements between two firms collaborat-
ing on a specific project. For example, a national firm that
specializes in stadium design may enter into a joint venture
with a local firm for a project on a college campus. Two
small firms may form a joint venture to pursue a project
that is larger than either firm could handle alone.

A joint venture is a partnership, and as a business entity,
functions like any other type of partnership. Any profits are
passed along to the partners, as are the tax liabilities. The
parties involved in the joint venture must determine how to
handle insurance; each firm may be covered by their respec-
tive liability insurance policy, or they may purchase a project-
specific policy for this venture.

AIA Document C101, *Joint Venture Agreement for Professional
Services*, may be used to establish the terms of the relationship.

72.   **The answer is C.**

The client's needs, project timing, and requirements of the
site would have the greatest impact on a cost analysis performed as a part of programming. The client's timing would
affect the time required for design and the project delivery
approach ultimately chosen for the project. Market conditions at the time of construction would be unknown during
programming and would likely be provided for with a contingency allowance.

73.   **The answer is B.**

The Urban Land Institute defines three types of shopping
centers. The amount of retail sales area provided and the
types of stores featured is determined primarily by the population of the catchment area. As a general rule, each person in the catchment area will support 3 ft² to 5 ft² (0.3 m²
to 0.5 m²) of retail space.

- *Neighborhood centers* provide daily convenience
  goods and services. Most have a grocery store or
  pharmacy as the anchor. Neighborhood centers
  serve about 7500 to 20,000 people within a six-
  minute driving radius. The center generally occupies about 4 acres to 10 acres (about 1.6 ha to 4 ha),
  with a building area of about 30,000 ft² to 75,000 ft²
  (about 3000 m² to 7000 m²) and an average building size of about 40,000 ft² (about 4000 m²).

- *Community centers* are often anchored by a large
  supermarket and often contain some type of variety
  store in addition to small services and specialty
  stores. This type of shopping center serves approximately 20,000 to 100,000 people. Community
  centers range in size from about 100,000 ft² to
  300,000 ft² (about 1 ha to 3 ha), with an average
  size of about 150,000 ft² (about 1.4 ha). The center
  generally occupies 10 acres to 30 acres (about 4 ha
  to 12 ha).

- The typical American shopping mall would be considered a *regional center*, as would a cluster of large
  "big box" retailers. Regional centers draw from a
  large geographical area and serve 100,000 to
  250,000 people, generally with an average building
  area of about 40,000 ft² (about 4000 m²). Total built
  area may range from 300,000 ft² (about 3 ha) to
  over 1,000,000 ft² (about 9 ha). The center generally occupies about 20 acres to 50 acres (about 8 ha
  to 20 ha).

74. The answer is D.

The calculations listed in options A, B, and D are a part of conducting a *life-cycle cost analysis*. *Uniform capital recovery* is used to calculate the annual value of a present value. Using a discount rate puts the future amount into terms of today's dollars.

Uniform present worth expresses a series of uniform annual amounts (such as an annual maintenance fee) in today's dollars. *Uniform sinking fund* is used to calculate the amount that would have to be invested today at a certain interest rate to have a specified amount of money at some point in the future (such as savings for a roof replacement in five years).

75. The answer is C.

Crime Prevention Through Environmental Design (CPTED) is a concept of the National Crime Prevention Institute. CPTED evolved from defensible space ideas. It relies on the inhabitants to police their own surroundings. The goal is to design an environment that encourages them to do so by clearly defining public and private spaces and by making streets, parking areas, and building entrances more visible to those who live in the area.

CPTED is focused on influencing behavior in positive ways through a neighborhood's design. Regulating behavior, such as by placing activities in particular locations, is outside its scope.

For more information on CPTED, see AIA Best Practices 17.07, *Understanding Human Behavior Leads to Safer Environments*, or *Crime Prevention Through Environmental Design*, by Timothy D. Crowe, available through the AIA Bookstore at www.aia.org.

76. The answer is B.

The *angle of repose* is the angle at which unconsolidated material sits at rest. A material's angle of repose is dependent on the surface area of the particles and its density, moisture content, and internal coefficient of friction. It is usually between 30° and 37°.

As an example, imagine building a sand castle at the beach. If you scoop up a bucketful of dry sand and pour it out into a pile on a level surface, the angle of the slope of the "hill" is the material's angle of repose. If the sand is slightly damp, the angle formed will be much steeper—possibly even vertical. But if the sand is very wet, it will behave more like a fluid and the angle formed will be much shallower.

77. The answer is A, B, D, and F.

Most zoning setback regulations affect buildings, accessory buildings, and their various components. These include bay windows, roof overhangs, and decks. However, some zoning ordinances are written to allow exceptions such as roof overhangs, if they don't project more than a certain distance into the setback, or decks that are close to the ground and do not include a roof structure. Landscaping and fences are generally excluded from setback requirements.

Each jurisdiction interprets setback requirements a little differently, so it is important to research the requirements governing a specific site.

78. The answer is A.

Elevating a structure on piles, piers, or columns preserves natural drainage patterns and allows a building to be constructed in areas prone to flooding, with unstable soil, or on a steep slope.

79. The answer is B.

The science of designing things and spaces so that they can be used most efficiently and comfortably by people is called *ergonomics*. Ergonomics considers the size and proportions of the human body and analyzes how people interact with an object or their environment, with the goal of making objects and spaces easier to use, safer, and more efficient.

80. The answer is B.

The series of books written by Christopher Alexander and his team in the 1970s—*The Timeless Way of Building, The Oregon Experiment,* and *A Pattern Language*—advocate an environmentally sensitive, human-focused approach to design, drawing heavily from vernacular historical precedent. Through selection of a series of patterns, Alexander's work is designed to allow nonprofessionals to influence the design of their environments.

Kenneth Frampton is an architectural historian; his best known work is *Modern Architecture: A Critical History*, originally published in 1980. William Peña's *Problem Seeking* (1987) is a classic text on architectural programming. Kevin Lynch's *The Image of the City* (1960) discusses how people interpret their environments and find their way through unfamiliar places by forming a mental image of a place.

81.   The answer is B.

Tony Garnier's proposal for a *cité industrielle* (1901-1917) represents a rethinking of some of the ideas expressed in Ebenezer Howard's *garden city* plan, developed around 1898. Garnier was trained at l'École de Beaux-Arts, and his classical training is reflected in the design of the city, with major axes connecting differently zoned areas of the city. The buildings depicted in the city are primarily made of reinforced concrete; Garnier proposed softening the harshness of the concrete with densely planted, tree-lined pedestrian paths throughout the city, complementing other means of transportation. He also provided for state-of-the-art transportation hubs and hygienic facilities. However, religious facilities were excluded completely from the plan.

82.   The answer is C.

Because they are very porous, silts and clays allow water to migrate above the water table on a site.

Fine-grained soils are more likely to be affected by freezing and thawing than coarse-grained soils. Organic soil is never a suitable material for foundation support. Footings should always be placed below the frost line to protect them from the effects of freeze/thaw heaving.

83.   The answer is B.

An elongated form stretched along the east-west axis would be the most appropriate choice for a hot, humid climate. This shape would minimize east and west exposure. Overhangs or courtyards could be used to provide shade and enhance the cooling effects of the wind.

A square form is best suited to cold regions. A square or compact shape with courtyards is a good match for hot, arid regions. Rectangular buildings work well in temperate zones.

84.   The answer is D.

Shuttle diplomacy is the act of revising a written document over and over until two parties can agree on its contents. This process is lengthy and time-consuming but can be effective when two groups are very far apart in their opinions on an issue and there is a lot of contention. The programmer can serve as a neutral third party and attempt to negotiate a compromise.

Groupthink is the phenomenon of "decision by deference." It generally results in a mediocre product because issues are glossed over and everyone in the group adopts the thinking of the leader without challenging the validity of the ideas presented and seeking alternatives.

Brainstorming and lateral thinking are both idea-generating processes. *Brainstorming* encourages participants to generate as many ideas as possible with little regard for their feasibility and with no critiques of ideas allowed. *Lateral thinking* is nonlinear thinking that creates a number of alternatives for later evaluation.

85.   The answer is D.

New urbanism is an approach to town planning advocating more diverse housing opportunities and less dependence on cars. It is a reaction to "suburban sprawl," which is characterized by congested roadways, developments of "cookie cutter" houses, and wasteful use of land and resources. New urbanism is sometimes referred to as "smart growth," and the primary force behind the movement is the Congress of the New Urbanism (www.cnu.org), which has compiled the basic tenets into the *Charter of the New Urbanism*. A link to this document can be found at **www.ppi2pass.com/AREresources**.

Hallmarks of new urbanism include

- mass transit within walking distance of homes and businesses

- mixed-use zoning: multi-family housing, single family housing, and commercial uses in proximity to one another

- a blend of single-family homes and apartments in the same neighborhood; this allows people to choose a housing type that fits their needs so they are not forced to relocate out of the neighborhood as their needs change

- more independence for those who cannot drive or do not own a car

- narrow streets and frequent 90° intersections, to encourage drivers to be alert and make pedestrian paths safer while making the neighborhood easier to navigate

- on-street or small-lot parking rather than vast parking lots, which encourages more interaction between the businesses and the street and also reduces impervious area on the site

PRACTICE EXAM: VIGNETTE SOLUTION

SITE ZONING: PASSING SOLUTION

This vignette requires that the examinee determine the maximum site development area in plan view and the maximum buildable area in both plan and section. It also requires the examinee to interpret contour lines in plan and draw a grade profile from them.

Solving Approach

Step 1   Using the *sketch line* and *sketch circle* tools, block out the required setbacks and other restrictions. Draw with the sketch grid turned on. It is usually best to start with the requirements for the site development area. When setting back from irregular areas, draw multiple circles with a diameter equal to the setback requirement. Be especially careful of small areas that may be included in a larger setback restriction.

Step 2   Using the *sketch line* and *sketch circle* tools, block out the buildable area.

Step 3   Draw the final shape and size of the buildable area using the sketch lines as a guide.

Step 4   Draw the grade profile line using the appropriate tool. It is helpful to use the full-screen cursor to do this. Be sure to draw the profile at the section cut line.

Step 5   Using the *sketch line* tool, draw the vertical lines representing the buildable area at the section cut line.

Step 6   Using the *sketch line* tool, draw the various height restrictions based on the program requirements.

Step 7   Using the *sketch line* tool, draw the diagonal line representing further restriction on the maximum building height. Be very careful to start exactly where the program says to start.

Step 8   Using the *building profile* tool, draw the entire maximum building area following the sketch lines.

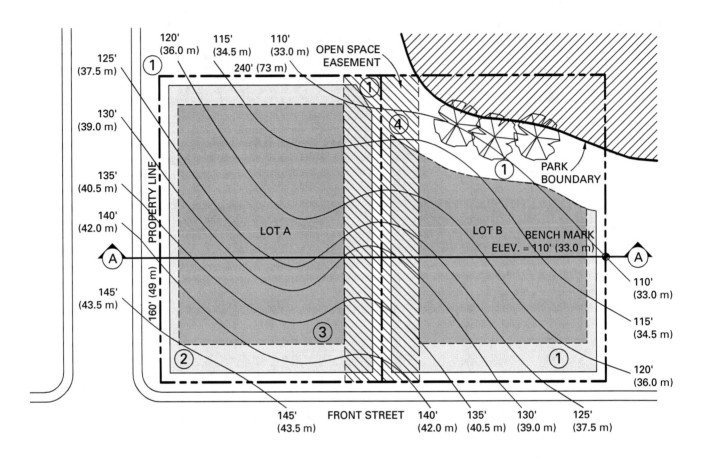

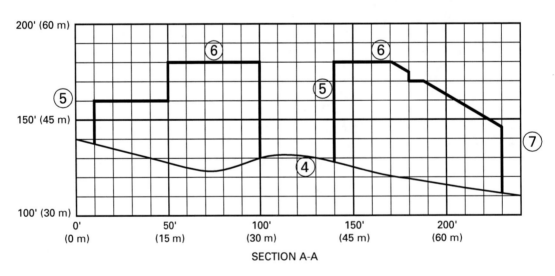

SECTION A-A

Scale: 1" = 50'-0"
(1:625 metric)

SITE ZONING:
PASSING SOLUTION

SITE ZONING: FAILING SOLUTION

Pitfalls

Note 1 — This plan fails to show a small portion of the site development area at the northeast portion on Lot A that is cut off by the required setback from the park boundary line.

Note 2 — The side setback of the buildable area along the property line separating the two lots is incorrectly shown as 5 ft (1.5 m) from the easement line instead of at the line of the open space easement.

Note 3 — The incorrect buildable line in plan view is carried into the section view.

Note 4 — The maximum height of the building on Lot A is incorrectly measured from the grade at the building line instead of from the grade at the *property* line as required in the program.

Note 5 — The diagonal building limit line is incorrectly started at a point along the building line instead of directly above the benchmark.

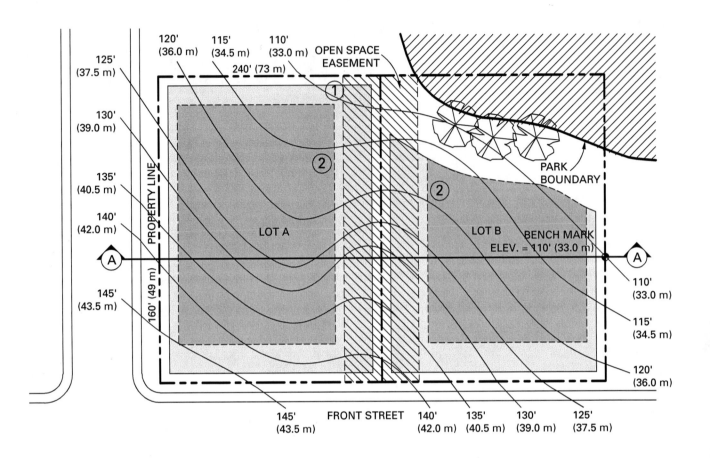

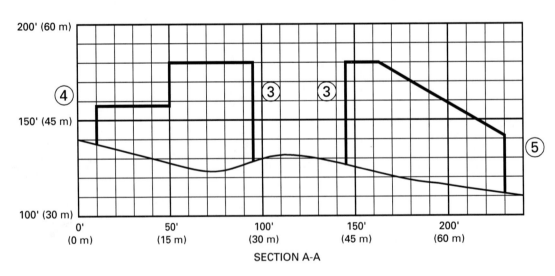

SECTION A-A

Scale: 1" = 50'-0"
(1:625 metric)

SITE ZONING:
FAILING SOLUTION